Metallica

METALLICA

The Frayed Ends of Metal

CHRIS CROCKER

St.
Martin's
Press
New York

Design by Jaye Zimet

Library of Congress Cataloging-in-Publication Data

Crocker, Chris.
   Metallica : the frayed ends of metal / Chris Crocker.
     p.   cm.
   ISBN 0-312-08635-0 (pbk.)
    1. Metallica (Musical group) 2. Rock musicians—United States—
Biography. I. Title.
ML421.M48C7   1993
782.42166'092'2—dc20
  [B]   92-33808
                                                  CIP

First Edition: January 1993

10 9 8 7 6 5 4 3 2 1

To my wife, who gave me love, laughter, patience and support. And to whom I taught the meaning of expressive sighing, frenzied inactivity, chihuahua nerves and why headphones were invented.

C O N T E N T S

ACKNOWLEDGMENTS

First thanks to helpful, brilliant and understanding friends Michelle Green, Jim Lyons, and the man who started it all, Ed Ryan.

Incredibly heartfelt and affectionate thanks to *la suprema* Metallica maven Nona Tallada, who was always there when I needed her—and often before. (*True Metallifanz vacation in L.A. during the riots!*)

Massive thanks and endless gratitude to Sue Brisk, who sees to it that I'm safe on the subways.

And a whole crocka love from the promoters of Paper Jam '92 to dear friends and astute colleagues and people who didn't know me from Adam but who helped me anyway: Brian Slagel; Jon and Marsha Zazula; Metal Maria Ferrero; Michael Alago; Michael Salomon; Lee Abrams; Harold DeMuir; Eddie McSquare; Bruce Haring; Marianne Meyer; Alexis Thompson; Larry "Because It's Louder" Lachmann; Steve "Dr. Rock" Kanengiser; Scott Schinder; Annene Kaye; Stephen Zukowsky; Miriam Lockshin; Melinda Newman; Paul Verna; Geoff Mayfield; Phyllis Stark; Susan Nunziata; Ed "The Mosher" Christman; Larry Flick; Ira Robbins; Jane Friedman; June Honey; Dorothy "Metal Mama East" Wheeler; Zita "Metal Mama West" Zukowsky; Cathy Coffey; Madeleine Morel; that guy at Revolver Records who unsealed all those magazines for me; Dr. Forster for keeping me on the medication; Jim, Alex and Lotte at St. M's; and Terry, Marilyn and

Cathy (who had to listen to me gripe for who knows how long). And a final thanks to the National Aeronautics and Space Administration, without whose assistance this book would not have been possible.

Chris Crocker writes exclusively on Leading Edge computers and IBM software.

A c k n o w l e d g m e n t s

I was a sweet young thing once
Now I'm a full grown crank
And when I die I'll probably come back
as a Sherman tank
—Todd Rundgren, "Heavy Metal Kids"

Metallica

INTRODUCTION

When heavy metal collided with the eighties, it made a booming, chaotic, foundation-rattling racket. Babies started to cry, chunks of ceiling plaster fell to the floor, and the cat disappeared for three days. Nobody was quite ready for it when heavy metal collided with the eighties.

Meanwhile, trillions of light-years out in space, what's left of the Big Bang looked over its shoulder to see what made all that noise. Oh. It was heavy metal colliding with the eighties.

Metal. Heavy. For people who want their music to be harder than rock—and a better conductor of electricity, too.

Metal is a music whose values are absolute—expressed to all in the *lingua franca* of sheer, eardrum-battering power.

Although it started out as the leaner, louder stepson of hippiedom, by the late seventies heavy metal had devolved into a stiff, lumbering beast, mired in tar pits of excess and self-indulgence. When the eighties hit like an unscheduled meteor, the dinosaur very nearly became extinct.

But then heavy metal—as in a thousand direct-to-video horror movies—*underwent a hideous mutation!*

The ghastly blotches that had appeared on its weathered visage were but a prelude to the greater abominations that followed. In the eighties, metal underwent a skin-shredding, stomach-churning shape-shift—the kind of ungodly, wrenching transformation dreamed of only on Freddy Krueger's Elm Street.

But it was *the eighties* that heavy metal collided with, after all. The eighties were a pretty rough neighborhood. The decade that left poor old heavy metal crumpled on the pavement like a pensioner mugged by hoodlums was the same decade that brought attacks on minorities, attacks on the poor, attacks on song lyrics, attacks on airliners, attacks on Grenada, attacks on Libya, defeat in Lebanon, dirty deals in Iran, dirty wars in Central America and disregard in government. Yes, when heavy metal collided with the eighties, heavy metal was in for quite a shock.

Think tanks and foundations calibrated just *how much* of a shock for us all the eighties were. The Center for the Study of Social Policy's 1992 report stated bluntly that America's children were worse off than they'd been ten years before. Across forty states, there was a 22 percent increase of children living in poverty, and a 56 percent rise in teen homicides. The ranks of teenaged mothers also swelled another 14 percent during that decade.

The eighties—like so many other special events—just weren't as good as the capsule description in *TV Guide* made them out to be. What began with the remunerative promise of The Greed Decade finished up gasping for air as The Frayed Decade.

And when officialdom made its periodic assessments of What's Going Wrong, heavy metal provided a hairy, beer-swilling, tattooed scapegoat—too busy having a good time to see what was coming. In the eighties, metal received the unwanted attention of ambitious politicians, reactionary pundits, self-styled religious revivalists and overzealous prosecutors. American society was being split between those who thought heavy metal was killing kids and the kids themselves—who had a pretty good guess that heavy metal was actually something to live for.

Parents who started giving serious thought to the idea that their kid might be an alien from outer space would be shocked to discover that the kid himself felt inclined to agree. If this kid needs anything, he needs his tunes. And desperately.

Metalheads don't have a political party. Like the libertarians, they're all over the place. They've sung for and rallied around "liberal" causes of reversing racism and stopping censorship. On the other hand, the fighter jocks of Operation Desert Storm were also cranking the metal, pumping themselves up before their next deadly run.

Whatever their persuasion, the heavy metal kids followed the Pied Powerchord in hopes that it might show them a way out of their predictable, stage-managed lives.

Metal in the seventies meant a lot to its fans. By the eighties, the stakes were even higher. By the eighties, metal had to unleash enough destructive energy to keep the kids themselves from exploding.

Parents were never quite comfortable with the heavy heraldry of thunderbolt-hewn AC/DC or Teutonic Motörhead, but these new-metal kids were something else. Devoting entire algebra classes to outlandish, ballpoint-pen pictograms, they'd replicate their icons: angular Anthrax, sacrilegious Slayer, stainless-steel Megadeth ... and one particular, singularly forbidding, barbed logo.

Metallica.

Metallica? What's the big deal? Aren't they just another heavy metal band?

Well, are they really? Could one heavy metal group,

unself-consciously shake their fans out of apathy and into passion—even as they led them out of childhood and into adulthood?

Metallica could.

Frayed not?

Frayed so.

When heavy metal collided with the eighties, the violent force of that impact formed a new element: Metallica. Like an angry demon awoken after aeons, Metallica rose up from nowhere to claim its multitudes. Behind a phalanx of snarling guitars, Metallica is unstoppable. And relentlessly, Metallica drives onward to conquer the nineties.

Heavy metal kids need their rock'n'roll to be visceral, even a tad violent. They need a band that *rocks*—powerfully, intelligently and tirelessly. And above all, honestly.

Metallica. It started out as a cult, and ended up a part of the culture.

> There's very few outside factors involved. It's not your typical 'Give the people what they want' or 'Yeah, we're here to play rock'n'roll for you and party all day' or any of that bullshit. This is fuckin' *our* shit, and we wanna do what's right for us, what we feel good about. If you like it, you're invited along. if you don't, well, there's the door.
>
> —Lars Ulrich, Metallica

1

Heavy metal was born the first day a guitar was used not as a musical instrument, but as a deadly weapon. Kinks' leader Ray Davies's clipped, snotty-boy vocals were matched to just such angular, rasping guitars in their 1964 hit "You Really Got Me" and the next year's "All Day and All of the Night." Like people trying to shake sand out of their shoes, rock'n'roll guitarists everywhere tried to get that surf-music twang out of their guitars and re-create the Kinks' angry-sounding "buzz saw" effect.

As the sixties wore on, rockers started shrugging off conventional pop or blues structures, writing songs around heavy, fuzztone-cloaked riffs. Foremost was Cream, the quintessential power trio, composed of Eric Clapton, Jack Bruce and Ginger Baker. In between hard-rocking remakes of blues oldies, Cream would deal out crunching guitar grooves like "White Room" or "Sunshine of Your Love." Iron Butterfly's 1968 "In-A-Gadda-Da-Vida" is a monumentally heavy riff, topped off by Doug Ingle's baritone-from-hell vocals. Anticipating metal's nothing-succeeds-like-excess ethos, the psychedelicized LP version ran a full seventeen minutes.

If some tattooed, leather-jacketed archaeologist wanted to unearth the missing link of prehistoric metal, he might end up digging Blue Cheer. Managed by an ex–Hell's Angel, Blue Cheer's enveloping, mondo distorto guitars could—and did—clear out the Fillmore auditorium. Barely visible behind their equally enveloping hair, Blue Cheer were allegedly confessed drug addicts. (In the sixties, drug addiction could still be considered a public relations plus.) But, to their credit, the noisemerchants in Blue Cheer were also the first American band to champion that fabled amplifier of the gods, the Marshall.

And, naturally, no history of heavy metal can be told without the towering presence of Jimi Hendrix, the self-taught genius who single-handedly reinvented the electric guitar. His hard-driving power trio expressed his blues and jazz influences with heavy rock riffs, colored by a never-before-heard arsenal of feedback, wah-wah effects, explosions, white noise and those peculiar sounds a guitar makes when it's being mangled, smashed, twisted or set on fire. (With Hendrix, the guitar was a weapon and a victim at the same time.) So great was Hendrix's wailing vision, he's become an idol to every successive generation of metal guitarists, even into the third decade after his death.

The term *heavy metal* is said to have first appeared in William Burroughs's 1959 landmark avant-garde novel *Naked Lunch*. It doesn't. His 1962 follow-up, *The Ticket That Exploded*, does contain a number of references to "heavy metal." While having nothing to do with rock'n'roll, they somehow convey the right atmosphere.

When Steppenwolf sang about "heavy metal thunder" in their 1968 hit "Born to Be Wild," it may have put a bug in the ears of those fans or rock critics who put the term to use. The biker-identified regalia of metal was anticipated by the hippie road movie *Easy Rider,* which featured "Born to Be Wild" as something of a theme song. (Of course *Easy Rider* was about *hippie* bikers, who were more into smoking grass than kicking ass, but its themes of freedom and social defiance have remained.)

Led Zeppelin started out as four English lads (Robert Plant, Jimmy Page, John Paul Jones and John Bonham) who sincerely wanted to play the blues but who just couldn't get it right. Unable to master the wincing nuances of traditional bluesmen, Led Zeppelin bludgeoned the blues and told everybody they *meant* to do it that way. But when Led Zep wasn't taking a jackhammer to blues traditions, they were creating increasingly original and elaborate uses of this new heavier rock'n'roll sound. Over the course of ten albums, Plant's inscrutable, wiry vocals and Page's roaring guitar blasted out instant classics from the over-the-edge boogie of "Black Dog" to the lavish rock orchestrations of "Stairway to Heaven" to the otherworldly riffsmanship of "Kashmir." Led Zeppelin will probably remain the most influential metal band of all.

In distinct contrast to Led Zeppelin's unfettered, rainbow-hued explorations, the Birmingham-bred four-piece named for the Boris Karloff movie *Black Sabbath* appeared in 1970 to give the Devil his due. With the classic lineup of Ozzy Osbourne, Tommy Iommi, Geezer Butler and Bill Ward, Black Sabbath dwelt in the darker, murkier, more occult pathways of rock. Black Sabbath's importance to heavy metal can be heard everywhere—in the triumphant crunch of "Paranoid," the ritualistic chant of "Iron Man," or the grief-rattled guitars of "Killing Yourself to Live."

After Ozzy's split with the band in 1979, the Sabs'

frontman was the operatic Ronnie James Dio, then Deep Purple alumnus Ian Gillan. The Sabs kept rocking into the nineties under the leadership of remaining member Iommi.

The third pillar of classic metal is Deep Purple, a bell-wether rock group. The indispensability of Deep Purple can be heard on their ground-breaking metal albums from the early seventies, *Deep Purple in Rock* and *Machine Head*. One of the first to incorporate classical harmonies into their music, Deep Purple had no shortage of such high-voltage rockers as "Black Night," "Child in Time," and their all-time megariff monster hit "Smoke on the Water."

After one of Deep Purple's numerous personnel changes, guitarist Ritchie Blackmore formed the seminal seventies metal band Rainbow, launching the career of future Sabbath vocalist Dio.

In the middle of the seventies, glam-metal rockers like Queen, Sweet, T. Rex, Slade, and later, Kiss, would keep the world safe for flamboyant clothes and makeup, androgyny, bizarre theatrics and powerful riffing.

Two standard-bearers of seventies metal tradition were K. K. Downing and Rob Halford, the guitar-and-vocals team of Judas Priest. Their 1976 album *Sad Wings of Destiny* proved that Black Sabbath wasn't the only metal band of the day to give the cauldron of occultism a good stir. Later in the decade, Halford switched to his biker-leathers metal-stud-overload persona, and the band would serve as the precursor of the wave of metal that would spill out of England and swamp the world in the eighties.

Germany's Scorpions were another favorite metal act of the seventies, and featured two guitar virtuosi: meister-slinger Michael Schenker and the Hendrix-mystic Ulrich Jon Roth. Schenker would later leave to join UFO, and brother Rudolf Schenker took his place in the Scorps.

As rock musicians became more sophisticated and better trained, they had an undeniable urge to share their musical sophistication with the public at large—sometimes not a very good idea, leading previously compelling bands to lose themselves in self-important noodling.

At its best, progressive metal took virtuoso musicianship and orchestral intimations to new heights, sometimes incorporating other seventies elements, such as jazz-rock or electronics. Canadian trio Rush made metal on a grand, nearly Wagnerian scale, and their albums were often elaborate concept pieces. One of Rush's most influential projects was the science fiction–themed *2112*, released in 1976.

One sixties band that grew into a seventies prog-metal institution was a crew of psychedelic rockers called Hawkwind. Their progressive metal-delia retained a strong, if somewhat trippy, audience even into the eighties.

Hawkwind's greatest contribution to metal came from somebody they fired. When they dumped their bass player Lemmy Kilmister in 1975, he was left with no choice but to form Motörhead. With guitarist Fast Eddie Clarke and drummer Philthy Animal Taylor in their classic lineup, Lemmy and Motörhead fired the opening volley to a metal revolution. Their bone-rattling, gamble-for-your-life-themed "Ace of Spades" was a relentless rocker of pivotal importance. The band even got a British hit mauling "Louie Louie."

On the other side of the world, in Australia, the Scottish-born Young brothers founded a determinedly hard-rocking group known as AC/DC. Although their sound shifted somewhat when lead singer Bon Scott died and was replaced by Brian Johnson, they put metal in an exalted place. Their best-loved rockers include the crashing, anthemic licks of "If you Want Blood (You've Got It)" and the twenty-one-gun salute of "For Those About to Rock." Like Motörhead, their angry vitality convinced some listeners that they were a punk band, but far from it—AC/DC would ultimately become arguably the most reliably rocking metal band of all time.

While these metal flame-bearers drove on towards newer and nastier riffs, prog-rock was growing out of control, like some science fiction fungus. A crime of overblown, self-important prog-rock just too horrible for words was Emerson Lake & Palmer's *Works* (in Volumes I and II, naturally). A collection of rambling solo projects with an unneeded symphony orchestra, the ludicrous excesses of ELP stood as a symbol of everything that was wrong with rock'n'roll in the late seventies. If ever there was a corrupt regime for young rock'n'rollers to rail against, this was it.

The revolution did come to rock music, and it came under the arbitrary name of punk. In the U.S. and U.K. during those years, a bunch of energetic, frustrated and usually musically inept bands rose up against the guitar virtuoso/prog-rock ideal. They became, quite arbitrarily, punks, whose regressive, basic rock style was as gripping as it was inarticulate.

Proudly planting themselves outside the rock business establishment, the punk–New Wave movement encompassed a multiplicity of genres, but the bands shared one important trait: they had to release their music on their own independent labels. The indie album world created by punk was a wonder of underground entrepreneurship, and its creative infusion gave the major-league record industry a creative transfusion. Such labels as Stiff, Slash, Rough Trade, SST, Twin Tone and Ace of Hearts released a broad range of alternative rock music.

Some of those bands did little to conceal their metal allegiances. One classic punk-era New York outfit was the

Dictators, whose raucous punk-metal fusion on such songs as "Two Tub Man" was an indication of metal-crossbreeding to come. Dictators guitarist Ross the Boss Funicello went on to become the guitar-soul of Manowar, while their bassist Mark the Animal Mendoza later rouged it up as bassman for metal-glamsters Twisted Sister.

But by the end of the seventies, the British heavy metal kids wanted to know how come punk was getting all the attention, and they sought to emulate groundbreakers Priest, Motörhead and AC/DC. As 1980 rolled around, metal bands were starting to appear all over England, playing louder and harder than their forebears. The lessons of the punks weren't lost on these young metal guns. They would put out their own albums on independent record companies, and labels such as Neat, Bronze, Rondolet and others were ready to thrust new metal into the daylight.

Geoff Barton, a writer for British rock weekly *Sounds*, dubbed these upstart metal bands the "new wave of British heavy metal." This resulted in the clumsiest acronym in recent memory—NWOBHM—but he who names it first usually names it for good, and Barton's term stuck.

Tygers of Pang Tang were one of the first NWOBHM bands to gain massive popularity on Neat, with a classic lineup in effect for only their first album *Wild Cat,* after which lead singer Jess Cox left the band. Their drummer's name was supposedly Brian Dick, but he sometimes went by the nickname Big.

Iron Maiden started in London in 1976, and after years of gigging around, they landed an opening spot with the European Kiss tour and a deal with EMI Records. Purists will prefer the two albums recorded with lead singer Paul Di'Anno, who was replaced by a Samson vocalist named Bruce Bruce. Returning to a less redundant form of his name,

Bruce Bruce became Bruce Dickinson became the voice of the Maiden from *The Number of the Beast* onwards. Maiden's decomposed-wraith-from-beyond-the-grave mascot Eddie has become one of the most recognized symbols of metal—and another sign of the heavy metal–horror movie connection.

On the pop side of the NWOBHM, Def Leppard came out of Sheffield in the late seventies, and since their stunningly successful 1983 *Pyromania* album, they've achieved a global following and lost most of their heavy metal credibility along the way.

Angel Witch, a mystically influenced power trio that released only one album, played edgy, hypertense metal. Angel Witch drummer Dave Dufort was the brother of Denise Dufort, who drummed for Girlschool, one of the few female metal bands to be repected by most of the metal community. Girlschool established themselves as the distaff Motörhead when they recorded the "St. Valentine's Day Massacre" single with Lemmy & Co.

Holocaust was a Scottish quintet that gained notoriety from its manager, who proved an interesting point to the record companies: he mailed bogus demos of already recorded, well-selling bands to record labels, which promptly dismissed the bands as not worth signing. This provided impetus to such bands as Jaguar, which launched its career by a six-song demo tape that was available to fans through mail-order.

Another heavily occult-oriented band was Witchfynde. Post-breakup hype created unsubstantiated reports that certain Witchfynde members had left as a result of unnamed dark forces in action.

A band that was no stranger to the witching hours was Venom, another NWOBHM act on Neat, but one with a presciently dark and speedy vision. Its members were known only by the names Cronos, Mantas and Abaddon. The band went to loony extremes in their occult metal antics, with such songs as "In League with Satan." Although something of a joke all along, Venom rocked viciously, if somewhat artlessly, influencing a generation of thrashers in the making.

To many of these NWOBHM bands, their crucial influence came not from Led Zeppelin, but from the sludgier grooves of Black Sabbath. In the same way that the punks looked past the more "influential" bands like the Beatles or the Rolling Stones and drew their inspiration from the lesser-known Velvet Underground, the new metal kids found Sabbath to be the dark beacon they needed to lead them into the eighties.

Back in the USA, metal took a back seat to overly mannered New Wavers like DEVO and the Talking Heads. Still, there were a few torchbearers left, and L.A. was their home turf. A local band called Mammoth took the last name of two of its members and became Van Halen. Although Kiss-er Gene Simmons produced their demo, it was live performing that landed them a deal with Warner Bros. Records, home of Deep Purple and Black Sabbath. Mostly a hard-rock band with strong metal tendencies, Van Halen's attraction was chiefly the ever-more-inventive, convention-defying guitartistry of Eddie Van Halen. As always, a transcendent guitar whiz would pull in the metal maniacs. An average metal band like Quiet Riot became a sensation on the strengths of *their* lead guitarist, divinely inspired soloist Randy Rhoads, who would die tragically in a small-airplane crash in 1982.

Glam-metal—despite the battering its image took from the increasing cartoonishness of Kiss and from lesser lights such as the unendurable, self-parodying prettyboys Angel—began to take root in Los Angeles. Glam revivalists

Angel—began to take root in Los Angeles. Glam revivalists Mötley Crüe (whose debut album *Too Fast for Love* was released on their independent Leathur label before Elektra signed them) showed the harder, darker side of glam. In fact, it was the Glam Guignol of Alice Cooper that became something of a model for his latter-day followers. Alice truly received the sincerest form of flattery from the maniacal, misogynistic metalloids in W.A.S.P.

Despite all this activity, the newest metal of all was yet to be created. And a garage in the L.A. community of Norwalk was about to become its birthplace.

2

The average guy living in ninth-century England was abrasive, shaggy, rude, illiterate and stewed to the gills with mead. With credentials like that, a broadax-wielding Anglo-Saxon would have made a pretty good metalhead. And they had a word in Old English that never survived into Modern English. but should've: *béorscipe*.

Béor, the Anglo-Saxons' word for *beer*, was central to Old English life and so it comes first. *Scipe* meaning a strong personal bond, became "ship," as in *friendship* or *fellowship*. The Anglo-Saxons reveled in their *béorscipe*. Clearly party people, they were very serious about quaffing mead, getting rowdy, singing, telling epic tales and clattering their tankards together in friendship—or more accurately, *béorscipe*.

And so, with somewhat faulty logic, our story begins in *another* land founded by *another* shaggy, rude, drunken, broadax-wielding Germanic tribe: Denmark.

* * *

One Dane in particular concerns this story: Lars Ulrich, brought into the world in Copenhagen the day after Christmas, 1963.

Lars was the son of Torben Ulrich, who ran a jazz club in the fifties, and was himself a sometime jazzman and jazz critic. He played little Lars jazz albums by the legendary likes of Miles Davis and Charlie Parker.

Torben Ulrich's principal occupation throughout the sixties and seventies was as a professional tennis player. He developed a reputation on the international circuit as a "hippie," in contrast to the country-club backgrounds of so many on the tennis scene. Lars remembers his parents as exceptionally open-minded, and they brought Lars all over the world as his father followed the tennis circuit. (Years later, Lars recalled, "I traveled more before I was ten than I have with Metallica.")

In February of 1973, Lars's father invited out a crew of friends who were in town for a tournament. At the same stadium their tennis was being played, Deep Purple was scheduled to give a concert. Torben Ulrich had landed five passes for his five friends. When one begged off at the last minute, little Lars was given the ticket to his first rock concert. Swamped by the massive Purple sound, Lars stared at Ritchie Blackmore flailing around the stage, pulling off fiery lick after lick. He'd never seen anything like it. The very next day Lars beelined for the record store and bought Deep Purple's *Fireball*.

After that, Lars and his friends had a pretend Deep Purple in Lars's bedroom—with a broomstick for Ian Gillian, tennis rackets for Blackmore and Glover, and a table soccer game for keyboardist Jon Lord. Lars, perhaps sensing the imperceptible pull of destiny, became a cardboard-box Ian Paice with paint stirrers for drumsticks.

With the intention of following in his father's footsteps,

Lars worked at intensive tennis training and became a ranked junior player. But a full schedule of practice and tournaments was wearing heavily on a kid who knew that *other* kids had time to hang out with their friends.

Listening to rock'n'roll was Lars's only escape from an eight-hour-a-day tennis regimen, his only rebellion against his strictly ordered life.

By 1977, a now-teenaged Lars got down on his knees before an understanding grandmother and begged for a *real* drum kit. His grandmother granted his wish, Lars became the proud owner of The Instrument That Parents Hate Most, and he began banging away mercilessly. But before too long, Lars would have to pack up his kit. The Ulrichs were moving to Los Angeles, California.

Los Angeles, the sunny dream-city of the American consciousness, has always been part Hollywood myth. Aware of the stark contrasts between the tinsel and reality in Los Angeles, its residents are usually the hardest on the place.

Lars Ulrich had gone from one cosmopolitan area to another, but relocation wasn't his big problem. No more than six months after he landed in the United States, he was ignoring his tennis practice, and started down that well-worn path to perdition that's packed with long-haired kids listening to metal bands and smoking pot. The wide-eyed, naughtily grinning young Dane was also finding that the attentions of California girls were a lot more interesting than working on his backhand.

"There are lots of really good tennis players out there, and those guys seem to live, eat and breathe tennis," Lars told *Hit Parader*. "I always had other interests—like playing drums and listening to rock and roll. I guess the fact is that the life of a musician—staying up late and jamming 'til dawn—isn't the right life for an athlete." Lars also received frequent sports injuries as a junior tennis player, but his hopes that a musician's life would be less hazardous proved to be overly optimistic.

For metalheads like Lars Ulrich, Los Angeles was all wrong. The biggest local buzz was for punk or punk-oriented bands like Black Flag, the Circle Jerks, X, the Flesheaters, and a host of skinheaded sympathizers. Whenever people in L.A. talked about metal, chances were that they were talking about the overblown, ponderous sounds of bands like REO Speedwagon. Undiscouraged, Lars kept abreast of his metal heroes of the NWOBHM by rifling the import-record bins in the eclectic record stores. He bought an airmail subscription to British rock weekly *Sounds,* while friends in Denmark and England continued to send him new albums.

Elsewhere in the Los Angeles area, in the suburb of Woodland Hills, a young man named Brian Slagel was also busy seeking out what few NWOBHM albums he could from local record stores. "Back in 1981, there were basically . . . two people who were into the New Wave of British Heavy Metal scene that was going on," recalls Brian Slagel. "It was myself and a guy named John Kornarens. I met him at a music swap meet. He was wearing some metal shirt and we started talking. We were both really crazy about the scene happening in England. There was nothing going on in L.A. where anybody knew anything about it. We would have to scour the city for information."

Needlesss to say, whenever there was a European metal act booked at an L.A. venue, Brian and John would be there. "Michael Schenker played the Country Club out here and John and I both were at the gig," Brian remembers. "Afterwards, John saw this guy wearing a Saxon European T-shirt in the parking lot—walked up to him and said, 'Hey,

Lars and Dave strike a typical stance. *Courtesy Kevin Hodapp.*

where'd you get that?' and he said 'Oh, I just moved here from Denmark.' So they became friends."

With a palpable thrill of recognition, Lars, Brian and John would become brothers in metal fandom. "John and I went out to Lars's house about a week later," Brian explained. "We all became friends because we were the only three who were into the scene. We would drive two hours to record stores trying to find the latest single."

The year was 1981. Lars was seventeen and living with his parents. He got a job delivering the *Los Angeles Times* between three and five every morning. Brian Slagel was working at Sears, but eventually got a job at a small mom-and-pop record store. There, Brian induced the owners to start importing more of the metal albums that he, Lars and John craved. To the owner's pleasure, these records sold well, and the NWOBHM crew had a fresh supply of imported metal. But that wasn't enough for Lars Ulrich.

"Finally you get fed up with being in L.A. because there was nothing going on here," says Brian Slagel. "So Lars went to England for a few weeks and just hung out with Motörhead and Diamond Head and all these bands that we were really into."

Lars flew to London in 1981 with the intention of seeing Motörhead, Tygers of Pang Tang, Saxon, and his favorites, Diamond Head. "By reading stuff in *Sounds* and *NME* [*New Musical Express*] and all the magazines that were covering it at the time, you knew what was going even though you were however many thousands of miles away," says Brian. "Lars just went over there and found out through someone where Motörhead was rehearsing. He just went and hung out where the rehearsal room was. They came out and talked to him and he said 'I came over here from L.A. blah blah blah' and they said, 'Hey, come on in hang out with us.' "

But one of Lars's main objectives was to seek an audience with Diamond Head, a band formed in the late seventies by schoolmates in the town of Stourbridge in Britain's
West Midlands. With Sean Harris's impudent lead vocals
and Brian Tatler's ripsaw guitar riffs, Diamond Head recorded a series of NWOBHM classics, including the famed
Lightning to the Nations.

To meet Diamond Head, all of Lars's natural talents for
schmoozing and hanging out came into play. "He went to
go see Diamond Head," recalls Brian Slagel, "and back then,
these bands were playing little clubs, so you could go up
afterwards. If you wait around long enough, you can meet
the band. He ended up *staying* with those guys over there."
Brian Tatler has memories of Lars hanging around while Tatler
and Harris worked on their riff-laden arrangements. Tatler
suspected that during the month he lived with Diamond
Head, Lars was socking away his observations for future use.

When Lars came back from England, he had been
energized by this pilgrimage to the mecca of the NWOBHM.
With thoughts of actually forming a band of his own, Lars
called a guitarist he'd briefly jammed with before his trip.
His name was James Hetfield.

James Hetfield was born on August 3, 1963, in Los Angeles.
His father was a trucker raised in Nebraska and his mother
was a light-opera singer, who died when James was a
teenager. "My dad was always one of these 'Cut your hair!'
kind of guys. My mom was more open to things," James told
Faces years later. "She painted a lot. She kinda reminded me
of a Berkeley mom. She wasn't alive for any of my success
with Metallica. It really pisses me off. But you know, I think
she knows what's going on still."

James's brother David was ten years older and
adopted hippie attire. James thought David—a Deep Pur-

ple and Jethro Tull fan—was way cool. David Hetfield's band played Hendrix covers—among other things—and wore matching pin-striped suits with leather belts.

David was a drummer and an occasional guitarist, and his band used the Hetfield garage to practice in. Young James often picked up the musical instruments when the band wasn't around. An unattended drum set was a clear invitation for James to climb up on the stool and start slamming away. As James later told *Musician,* it was "something to make my mom mad."

As a schoolkid, James didn't find his studies especially stimulating, although he did have a special place in his heart for science class, with all the fun that could be had playing with the Bunsen burners or dissecting frogs.

James had a horror-movie fan's fascination with things morbid. In fact, it was the occult overtones of Black Sabbath that lured him into their curious, cobwebbed camp. Despite his clear musical preferences, James was coerced into taking piano lessons by his musically trained mother.

But James's discomfort with piano lessons was the least of his problems at home. James's father was a strict Christian Scientist. When James was little, he'd lie in bed on Sunday mornings pretending to be asleep—hoping that he'd get out of going to church.

School, too, was different for James. In accordance with Christian Science teachings against medicine, he would sometimes be treated differently than his schoolmates.

When the rest of his friends took health class, James would have to leave the room. (Health was probably no one's favorite course, but no child needs to feel he's being treated differently from the other kids.) Whatever the subject matter, James felt that things were being hidden from him that were revealed to the other students.

By the time James had entered high school, the Hetfields had separated, with James's father moving out of the house.

"When we used to go hang out over at Lars's house," recalls Brian Slagel, "he used to have an un-put-together drum set lying in the corner and he'd always go, 'I'm gonna start a band.' We're like: 'Yeah, sure you are, Lars. Yeah, right.'"

Before leaving for England, Lars actually had made moves towards starting a band. After searching for a metal-loving guitarist, he made contact with James. Their first ill-fated session together was bedeviled by a disobedient cymbal that insisted on falling over during the songs. James would stop while Lars set it up again.

When Lars got back from the U.K., he and James had better luck. James was working in a sticker factory, and Lars was delivering the *Los Angeles Times*. "When I got the band together, I just wanted to play," Lars told *Creem*. "It was really exciting just trying to be in a band. It was never 'Let's make it big!' or anything, it was simply a way out, a way of escaping the daily boredom. It was just a lot of fun to do."

James, who'd played in a couple of cover bands before meeting Lars, wanted to give up the guitar altogether. With the unbearable competition among L.A.'s legions of guitarists, he'd tried his hand at lead vocals. Singers didn't seem to be behind every rosebush as guitarists were.

James, whose solemn background leaned towards the working class, soon became close with the somewhat bohemian, world-traveled Lars. Both had a taste for metal, and both needed a pressure-release valve. James wanted to leave his strict homelife behind him for a while, and Lars needed to escape from the rigors of his cradle-to-the-grave sports regimen.

By the end of 1981, the Hetfield's living room had

become the as-yet-unnamed band's rehearsal space. A bass player was added with the recruitment of James's roommate Ron McGovney. Eventually, a guitarist named Lloyd Grant filled out the lineup. (Grant found himself in the lonely position of being a black musician on the nearly all-white L.A. metal scene.)

Any new band styles itself after its personal favorites, and Lars and James's whatever-we're-gonna-call-ourselves band was no exception. James, who got into classic metal after going through his brother David's album collection, was a fan of southern rockers Lynyrd Skynyrd. James also admired Malcolm Young of AC/DC, for his raw, pounding approach to rhythm guitar.

Lars has commented that when he met James, James had only just heard of Iron Maiden. Before long, Lars had made sure that the band learned his favorite songs by Judas Priest, Diamond Head, Motörhead, Angel Witch and Trespass, the NWOBHM band that released a series of fine melodic metal singles on U.K. independent Trail Records.

Lars's favorite guitarist was still Ritchie Blackmore, of Deep Purple and Rainbow, but as a drummer, he tried to emulate Motörhead's Philthy Animal Taylor. Lars would later tell the BBC: "What we got from Motörhead back in '80/'81 was the aggression and the energy and the speed that Motörhead had back then, around the *Overkill/Ace of Spades* albums. . . . That's why the band sounds so European. When I moved to L.A. in 1980, we wanted to get a band together that had a European-sounding background, and since I came from over there I had a lot of the influences with me, like Motörhead and other bands like Diamond Head and some of the other early New Wave of British Heavy Metal bands."

The first song James and Lars ever wrote together was entitled "Hit the Lights."

Brian Slagel, who up until that time had been editing a local fanzine called *The New Heavy Metal Review,* was thinking about a compilation album of young metal bands. His experience in record retail left him with contacts at such independent distributors as Important and Greenworld. (Independent distributors are the homemade label's only means of getting its albums into any record stores. The major record labels have their own distribution networks.) Brian's indie-distrib friends agreed that the project was a worthy pursuit, and Brian Slagel set about the task of gathering together the artists to fill out his roster of ravenous rockers. Many of the L.A. headbangers already knew Brian Slagel, who had been promoting local metal shows.

New L.A. metal bands were interested in Brian Slagel's project. So was Lars Ulrich.

"When I was putting together the album, he called me up," Brian remembers. "He was jamming with James and a couple other guys in their garages playing Diamond Head covers and everything. He said, 'Hey, if I put together a band and give you an original song, will you put it on the record?' And I said, 'Sure, of course.' So that was basically the beginning of Metallica."

And the compilation that would become *Metal Massacre* was also the beginning of Brian Slagel's Metal Blade Records. Metal Blade would grow from that point into one of the premier metal labels in operation.

Metal Massacre was the beginning of Metallica, but it was really more like the birth of jesus-we'd-better-think-of-a-name-for-this-band-someday. Then fate stepped in. As Brian Slagel explains, "Someone was forming a fanzine and they gave Lars a list of names and said, 'You're a metal guy, what do you think I should call it?' Lars saw 'Metallica' on there and said, 'Well, pick this other one.' He liked the name—so he called the band Metallica."

Brian Slagel won't suggest that there was larceny in Lars's adoption of the name Metallica, saying that Lars "*borrowed it*, let's say."

The man with the fanzine-name list was a San Franciscan metal maven named Ron Quintana. "I'd met Lars at shows and stuff in the city. We always talked about starting a band or opening a record store or even starting a magazine," Ron recalls. "We'd just shoot the shit and talk about names and stuff and we threw a lot of names together, but we never got around to doing anything."

Quintana's fanzine ended up with the name *Metal Mania*. Yet Ron doesn't begrudge Lars's appropriation of Metallica. "He had some really *bad* names himself," Quintana remembers with a laugh, "like Red Veg or Blitzer or something. I guess mine wasn't much better because I ended up with *Metal Mania*—which isn't very original, but it worked. We had all kinds of different names. Actually, he had his own list too and we would compare names. . . . It's funny. A few of them were even taken by bands."

When Lars, James, Lloyd and Ron recorded "Hit the Lights," they'd still never played a real gig, but they could whip up some high-energy rock. It's rumbling, opening fanfare is like a movie overture, welcoming you to suspend disbelief. Using violent imagery as a call to party, James's double-tracked vocals wail wild and long, like a gremlin from Hell. Gatling-gun guitar riffs discharge to a pogoing punk beat, like metal on speed. Lloyd Grant's jagged, hyperactive solo wrestles the song to a close.

When Lars and James handed Brian the rudimentary four-track tape of "Hit the Lights," he was astonished: "I was like, 'Wow, this is really amazing. I can't believe these guys have really gotten it together.' "

Not every hurdle had been cleared, however. When they brought the "Hit the Lights" four-track to the mastering studio, the engineer told them that their tape needed to be "bumped up" to a somewhat more professional reel-to-reel, at a cost of $50. A quick pooling of their resources paid the bill, and rock'n'roll history was allowed to proceed as scheduled.

Years later, Brian Slagel told *Hits,* "They probably would've stayed in their garage forever except they had this opportunity to do something."

The burgeoning L.A. metal scene documented on *Metal Massacre* was starting to raise international eyebrows. Brian and the newly named Metallica became friends with the correspondent for *Sounds,* and soon there would be a very good chance that the magazine Lars pored over every week would soon be poring over *him.*

Locally, homemade metal fanzines conveyed news of the mostly underground scene. Top bands of the day included Mötley Crüe, Ratt, Dokken, W.A.S.P. and Steeler, the latter a combo that featured Ron Keel—and would later showcase Scandinavian guitar whizkid Yngwie Malmsteen. And there was Bitch, a sometimes Motörhead-like four-piece led by a nice Jewish girl named Betsy Bitch (*née Weiss*). She routinely performed in leather dominatrix attire, but her mother was always somewhere nearby. Popular venues for the new metal bands were the Whisky, the Troubadour, the Country Club and the Woodstock in Anaheim.

By the early eighties, L.A. was establishing itself as the metal mecca for the entire country. Wild-maned rockers arrived thick and fast, their cars piled high with instruments, equipment and record collections.

The *Metal Massacre* compilation—which also included Ratt's debut track—was such a rousing success that *Metal Massacre* became a continuing series, consistently showcasing the freshest hot-out-of-the-smelter new metal. Other *Massacre* alumni were the Canadian metal progressive band Voivod and Armored Saint, a savagely rocking band that would record for Metal Blade into the nineties and stay together with very little change in personnel. In Metal Blade Records' first ten years, its signees have included DRI, Fate's Warning and the wild, bizarro-metal act GWAR.

In 1982, a new metal band from Orange County started getting gigs around town. Led by a singer-bassist named Tom Araya, they chose the name Slayer. While other bands half-heartedly dabbled in Sabbathesque occultism, Slayer's sonorities sounded like they were being fed through the Devil's own reverb. Joined by guitarists Jeff Hanneman and Kerry King and by drummer Dave Lombardo, Slayer's maniacal speedriffing and blatant demonic displays would earn the band widespread social disapproval—and ever-growing legions of fans.

Slayer's first recorded song appeared on *Metal Massacre III* in 1982. By 1983, Brian Slagel had released their debut album *Show No Mercy*. Metal Blade would release three Slayer albums before the band's switch to Def American Records, where they would cut the speedmetal landmark *Reign in Blood*.

When Lloyd Grant left Metallica, Lars and James placed an ad in the classifieds newspaper *The Recycler*. The ad was answered by a blond-haired, prodigiously talented lead guitarist named Dave Mustaine. Musically, Dave was from the same neighborhood as Lars and James—with favorite bands that included Iron Maiden, Judas Priest, Diamond Head, Angel Witch and Witchfinder General, another English occult-metal band that once stirred up controversy for an album cover that pictured a semiclad woman getting her throat slit over a gravestone. (A serious lapse in taste, even by metal standards.)

Dave remembered that the early days of Metallica were awash in peppermint schnapps, Mickey's Wide Mouths, vodka and tomato sandwiches. Lars, James, Dave and Ron, through the rigors of rehearsing and recording, formed a special bond—a *béorscipe,* you might say.

Bands like Slayer and Metallica had a long way to go before they conquered the nation—or even Los Angeles, for that matter. Metallica, for instance, still needed a gig. Fortunately, it wasn't long before they got one.

"Their first-ever gig was opening for Saxon," says Brian Slagel. "Saxon was playing four shows at the Whisky, and they decided to pick different local acts to open the show. So Metallica got this gig, and that was the first-ever show that they played. James didn't play guitar. Mustaine was the only one playing guitar. Their set basically consisted of Diamond Head covers and a couple other New Wave of British Heavy Metal covers. I think 'Hit the Lights' was the only original they did. They were a garage band at that point."

Even after their first gig, Metallica's search for a rhythm guitarist remained fruitless, with auditioning players either trying to overtake the lead guitarist or not having the aggressive attack Metallica needed. James reluctantly agreed to be lead singer and rhythm guitarist. His heavy downstroking style, copped from Tommy Iommi's thick Black Sabbath chordings, was perfect for the embryonic Metallisound.

Some of Metallica's first venues had a requirement for a band's set to be composed entirely of original songs. Since Metallica hadn't written enough songs to comply with this policy, they weren't exactly forthcoming about the origins of these catchy NWOBHM cover versions they played. While never telling anyone that they actually *wrote* these songs, they didn't actively discourage such beliefs.

Metallica's first songs drew energy from the dominant punk sound, but with the alloyed muscle of heavy metal. Of course, a more immediate reason for the speed and intensity of Metallica's metal was to shake up the somnolent audiences at their earliest gigs. The less responsive the crowd, the faster the tempos raced and the more James screamed into the mike like a punker.

This was not an approach appreciated by the people who booked acts at L.A.'s clubs. "The rock clubs wouldn't book us because they thought we were punk," James later told *Guitar Player,* "and the hardcore clubs would say, 'They're metal, they have long hair, get 'em out of here!'"

Metallica managed to get gigs opening up for bigger local acts, such as Mötley Crüe and Ratt, but Lars felt that Metallica was going to have a hard time fitting into their scene.

After starting to make it on the growing L.A. metal club circuit, Brian Slagel recalls that "they came to me at one point and said, 'Hey, let's do an album.' And I said, 'Well, do I have to spend money?' And they said, 'Well, we need eight thousand dollars to record a record.' I was a twenty-one-year-old kid at the time—I had no money." The newborn Metal Blade label wasn't quite ready to pay for an album's worth of studio time and production costs.

Instead of an actual album, the band set their sights slightly lower and agreed to record a demo tape. The demo was titled *No Life 'Til Leather.*

The band re-recorded "Hit the Lights," this time accented by Dave Mustaine's methodical madness on the outchorus guitar solo.

Six new originals followed, including Lars and James's "Seek and Destroy," which sang of a breed of relentless stalkers. The piercing, ten-note theme of "Seek and Destroy" is a classic embodiment-of-pure-evil soundtrack cue from a horror film. (On this recording only, James hits a metal-falsetto high note on his final *"Seek and destroy . . . !"*) Lars and James cribbed the song structure of "Seek" from an old Diamond Head tune. Lars was proving himself adept at mapping out the mechanics of a song, not just the riffs that flesh it out.

James's own composition "Motorbreath" is a fast-lane, life-affirming song, with muscular chords that hammer down the chorus. With James's heavily reverbed vocals, this jumpin' punk mazurka bears some resemblance to the music of horror-core rockers the Misfits.

The remaining songs were written jointly by James, Lars and Dave. Powered by a chugging guitar riff and a punkish flourish, "The Four Horsemen" is a classic metal theme of epic devastation and mystical terror given a biblical twist. (But somehow, these supernatural wraiths seemed to sport prison tattoos and carry hunting knives.)

"Jump in the Fire," told from the viewpoint of a beckoning demon, is marked by a mesmerizing guitar figure that ratchets up and down menacingly. Another heroic/demonic scenario is found in "Phantom Lord," whose opening chords seem to suggest another movie soundtrack (only with Lars's tom-toms being beaten in place of kettle drums).

And finally there was "Metal Militia," a Dionysian declaration of the metal life. The military imagery had its point—James's insane wailing was really a philosophical call to arms for the new metal.

No Life 'Til Leather was first circulated in 1982. Lars wanted the tape to be circulated as widely as possible. (There was that successful Jaguar tape that was delivered by mail.) He passed it out in hopes that it would circulate in the grass-roots network of metal aficionados. Lars knew that with widespread cassette copying, a small mailing of demos would grow algebraically across an informal demo-and-bootleg syndicate. Lars's only goal was to get Metallica a mention in a metal fanzine.

A record contract for Metallica? It was the furthest thing from their minds.

Now that Metallica had purloined a good name, settled their lineup and landed some local gigs, their path began to lead to other cities. "As part of a promotion for the *Metal Massacre* thing, we put together a show at the Stone in San Francisco, a *Metal Massacre* show," Brian Slagel recalls. "And it was gonna be Bitch, Metallica and Cirith Ungol, another local band that was on the *Metal Massacre* album. Cirith Ungol ended up dropping out 'cause they didn't have enough money to do it, but Bitch and Metallica went up to San Francisco and we played a show at the Stone."

The Stone's owner liked Metallica, and made sure to book the band again. But San Francisco had more to offer than just cable cars and great sushi.

"There was a band that was on *Metal Massacre II* named Trauma, who had this really amazing bass player," remembers Brian. "They played a show at the Troubadour one night and Lars and James were both there. They went berserk over this bass player, who turned out to be Cliff Burton."

While other accounts say that Lars and James first saw Cliff at the Old Waldorf in San Francisco, the powerful impression made by Cliff Burton was undeniable. And since their current bassist Ron McGovney wasn't working out as well as they'd hoped, the metal militia targeted Cliff Burton for recruitment.

Cliff Burton was born on February 10, 1962, in San Francisco, the son of Ray and Jan Burton. Cliff's musical abilities became evident as he grew up, and in his teens he played in local San Francisco bands EZ Street, Agents of Misfortune and A.D. 2 Million. Guitarist Jim Martin also played in these bands, and had been Cliff's friend since the late seventies. Jim enjoyed Cliff's intelligence and kindness as much as he was fascinated by his free-form musical inventiveness.

When Jim Martin decided to become a rock musician despite his parents' objections, Cliff Burton helped stiffen his resolve. One day Cliff saw Jim loading some lumber onto a truck with his bare hands—the kind of work where fingers could be easily crushed. Cliff cautioned Jim quite sternly, saying that as a guitar player, he'd be foolish to let his hands run such a risk. Cliff's concern was a needed confidence boost for Jim.

And when former EZ Street drummer Mike Bordin told Cliff that his new band Faith No More was looking for a guitarist, Cliff reminded Bordin of Jim Martin's availability. With Jim Martin on guitar, Faith No More have become hit-making, genre-bending alternative rockers, critically lauded as one of the most promising bands of the nineties.

* * *

By the time Metallica came courting, Cliff Burton was playing in Trauma, attending a local junior college and studying piano. Something of an unreconstructed hippie, Cliff was well-known for his distinctive, gleefully-out-of-fashion bell-bottoms. His literary tastes ran to horror, with H. P. Lovecraft a particular favorite.

Howard Phillips Lovecraft, who died in 1937 at age forty-six, wrote short stories and short novels in the twenties and thirties, most often published in the pulp magazine *Weird Tales*. Lovecraft's prose depicted rustic New England communities that shielded hidden worlds of subterranean pagan races, malevolent visitors from space and vengeful gods ready to burst forth and reclaim the Earth. His disbelieving protagonists often found explanations for these unearthly occurrences in the ancient volumes of dark knowledge found in the dusty stacks of Miskatonic University. On film, Lovecraft's bizarre themes were best served by the high-tech gore of eighties special effects, especially in the Stuart Gordon treatments of *The Re-Animator* and *From Beyond*.

Cliff's love of Lovecraft, which soon spread to the other members of Metallica, fit in well with the horror-movie subtexts of heavy metal. Under Cliff's influence, Lovecraftian themes would recur in the music of Metallica.

"The bass player was completely outrageous," Lars later told *Musician* of Cliff Burton. "We just looked at each other and said, 'That's our new bass player.'"

After their minds were made up that the pounding basslines of Cliff Burton's Rickenbacker belonged in Metallica, the next step was to get him to move down to Los Angeles. Lars, James and Dave spent four months trying to lure Cliff southward, but he wasn't budging. Finally, in a mountain-comes-to-Mohammed gesture, Lars, James and Dave all moved to San Francisco's East Bay area. They've lived there ever since.

Aside from having the band move hundreds of miles north, Cliff's musical influence on the band was profound. The best-trained musician in the band, Cliff taught harmony and music theory to Lars and James, proving to them that hard-driving metal need not be tuneless.

Cliff Burton was also responsible for opening his band-mates' ears to the melodic complexities of classical music. As Cliff once quite succinctly told *Sounds*: "Bach is God." Cliff also suggested that all the guys in the band had gone through Bach phases, except maybe for Lars.

The move to San Francisco separated Lars, James and Dave from their families, although their parents would also

James and Dave at an early East coast gig. *Courtesy Kevin Hodapp.*

leave Los Angeles. James's father eventually retired to live in Arkansas, and Lars's parents split up, with his mother relocating to Spain and his father heading north to Seattle. Lars's mother still sees the band when they're touring in her area, and his father continues to play jazz. "To this day, my dad . . . has still got longer hair than I do," Lars amusedly told *Spin*. "He's got a longer beard than the guys in ZZ Top. He looks like Rasputin."

San Francisco had been home to innovative rock bands ever since its sixties prominence as a psychedelic mecca, with such bands as the Grateful Dead, Jefferson Airplane, Quicksilver Messenger Service, Blue Cheer and Santana.

When the punk–New Wave movement heated up, San Francisco was again a creative magnet. The City by the Bay was home to such seminal alternative bands as the Avengers, the Readymades, Flipper, Tuxedomoon, the Residents, Snakefinger, the Nuns and an undefinable punk-metal combo called MX-80 Sound. Foremost on the San Francisco scene were the satirically inclined punks the Dead Kennedys.

The city's top venues included the Temple Beautiful and the Mabuhay Gardens (otherwise known as the "Fab Mab"), the latter a Filipino supper club turned punk palace.

When Cliff Burton was playing in Trauma, new metal bands started cropping up all over town. They included Vio-lence, Legacy and five teenaged Filipinos who'd go on to metal notoriety as Death Angel.

"When Metallica played L.A., people were under the impression they were a punk band, because they played a lot heavier and faster than more traditional metal bands," says Brian Slagel. "When we did this show up in San Francisco at the Stone, all of a sudden the kids really got into Metallica, more so than any of the other bands on the bill.

It was the first show that Metallica had done where they got a really great fan response. They were really happy."

San Francisco's reputation as a city built on tolerance was ringing true for Metallica. They even found the music scene to be less splintered. Bands of diametrically opposed genres seemed to remain friendlier to each other than in cliquish, trend-mongering L.A.

"There was a lot of glam rock going on . . . the Mötley Crües, the Ratts and Quiet Riots," James recalled to the *New York Daily News*. "We got up on stage and bashed away and people would scream, 'Get 'em outta here. Eek, they're all a bunch of punks.' Everyone was too worried about spilling their drink and looking around to see who else was in the club. Up in San Francisco, the kids were more open-minded and down to earth. They didn't care what anybody thought."

Or as Brian Slagel puts it, "The scene that started going on in San Francisco was much more the speed-thrash scene. You had bands like Exodus and Laaz Rockit and stuff. The kids were more into the harder-edged music up there."

One of the first San Francisco rock clubs that Metallica could call home was the Old Waldorf. On Monday nights—designated as heavy metal nights—Metallica was a permanent fixture.

San Francisco would hold other fond memories for the band, such as James's girlfriend. She was still living with her parents, yet James would still manage to sleep over. To avoid detection, James would tiptoe out of the house before sunrise and finish his night's rest in Golden Gate Park. On one groggy park-bench morning, James was awakened by a group of earnest-looking college students. They wanted to know about his life as a homeless person.

4

The brave new rockers of Metallica had no idea they'd be drawn to Cliff Burton's San Francisco, and they had no idea that yet another distant locale would affect them profoundly. There was little chance that even the world-traveled Lars Ulrich had visited this particular region. It was New Jersey.

The New York–area heavy metal scene was similar to that on the West Coast—a handful of metal believers trying to dig themselves out from under overhyped punk–New Wave dominance. The New York metalheads *did,* however, have one thing they could be thankful for: Jon and Marsha Zazula had quit Wall Street.

Married in the late seventies, native New Yorkers Jon and Marsha Zazula had used their combined backgrounds in finance and marketing to thrive in New York's competitive financial marketplace. But increasingly, the pressures of the market weren't worth it. With the money they'd accumulated, the Zazulas decided to settle back a bit and relax. "We basically were in a semiretirement from the madness of Wall Street and the Gold Rush. Just settling in to be normal people," Jon Zazula remembers, adding, "Just to supplement ourselves and keep ourselves interested, we started a little flea market operation."

In 1981, the Zazulas began their "flea market opera-tion"—a record store. Although Jon and Marsha's previous business was set in the land of pin-striped suits and non-stop telephones, their passion was for music. The bearded, bearish Jon had been a musician, and he remembers that Marsha had "one helluva record collection." Self-described products of the sixties, the Zazulas grew up listening to the great Motown artists as well as the cutting-edge rock of the day: the Doors, the Grateful Dead, the 13th Floor Elevators, Cream, Blue Cheer, the MC5, Quicksilver Messenger Service and the Cosmic Echoes. Their eclectic tastes extended into the jazz stylings of George Benson, Hubert Laws, Chick Corea, Grover Washington, and even the classical-jazz crossover of Jean-Pierre Rampal and Claude Bolling.

And so Jon and Marsha Zazula began their little record store (really only a set-aside corner of another record store) in the Route 18 Indoor Market in East Brunswick, New Jersey. Surrounded by the $180 worth of albums that was their initial investment, Jon and Marsha waited for a customer. And waited. And waited for several hours, in fact. Finally, someone bought a Springsteen import. And with this pur-chase was christened Rock N' Roll Heaven.

That their first sale was of an import album may have been some sort of retailer's omen—their imported product started selling like black plastic hotcakes. Rock N' Roll Heaven began to specialize in European picture discs and 45s, rare twelve-inch singles, EPs and imports of Brit pop faves like Depeche Mode or even Phil Collins. They also dealt in collectors' items like Springsteen picture discs or the discontinued flame-cover of Lynyrd Skynyrd's *Street*

Survivors album. They were selling Iron Maiden, but had no particular consciousness of the NWOBHM scene.

One day a young customer returned an LP—the first Angel Witch album. The Zazulas kept all their albums out in stock and had none for in-store play. They received no promo copies like the big record stores did. For lack of anything else to play, they put Angel Witch on the store's cheap stereo. And loved it.

Jon and Marsha's new interest in eighties metal was reflected in the bins at Rock N' Roll Heaven: Motörhead's *No Sleep 'Til Hammersmith* and *Ace of Spades*, Michael Schenker's *Live at Budokan*, the first EPs by Holocaust and Twisted Sister, as well as other releases from Venom, Girlschool, Bomber, Anvil, and more mainstream metal artists, like Rush.

"All of a sudden, the inventory in our place became Hellion and Riot and all these bands from left field," Jon recalls. "Everything on the Neat label and the Bronze label."

By carrying imports, promo items and collectibles, Rock N' Roll Heaven never had to compete with the big record stores that sold only mainstream domestic major-label product. By staking out their own corner of turf, the Zazulas found that the market for new metal was already big and starting to boom.

"There were no outlets for it," Jon Zazula explains, "and then everybody started to see how we grew from $180 worth of inventory—which was twenty-one records—to an inventory in seven months of $80,000." Before long, 90 percent of their stock was heavy metal. And they were making enough money to keep promos of their albums for hours of thrashing in-store play. They'd also made enough to buy out the guy who owned the booth, to further expand.

Jon and Marsha Zazula liked more than the disposable income of their young clientele—they liked the kids as well. "A lot of kids were coming in and buying the Motörhead, the Judas Priest, the Rush and we started talking," says Jon. "I was intrigued—and Marsha was intrigued—with the long hair, the denim jackets and the rebellious spirit of these kids.

"When Randy Rhoads died, Rock N' Roll Heaven became the mourning ground," Jon continues. "That night, there must have been seven hundred people in the store. Just there to come to us—just to be consoled. Their parents couldn't understand the devastation of losing Randy Rhoads. . . . Rock N' Roll Heaven by then had grown into this massive mecca for heavy metal people. They would travel five hundred miles to come and talk to us."

Aside from coming into Rock N' Roll Heaven looking for this-or-that-metal-album-that-somebody-told-'em-was-cool, the kids were asking why these bands never played in a big city like New York. Jon and Marsha had no answer for that. Motörhead and Bomber had toured the area, but they seemed like the only ones that did. Even metal bands from none-too-distant Canada—such as Anvil and Exciter—never got a gig in New York.

Jon and Marsha explored the ins and outs of promoting a rock concert—to do something for the kind of kids who filled their store. They started to learn about the immigration procedures necessary to bring foreign bands into the United States and the many intricacies of concert promotion.

"The first show we did was an Anvil show, which drew over a thousand people" to the on-site ballroom at the Route 18 Indoor Market, Jon Zazula recalls. "We *should've* made a lot of money on it. We *lost* money because we didn't have a clue and everybody took us to the cleaners, but we developed our name as promoters in the New Jersey area at that point."

And the heavy metal kids of the New York area finally got to hear Anvil (the Toronto-based four-piece power-house fronted by a lead singer named Lips). And thanks to the Zazulas, many in the crowd were already familiar with Anvil's hard-rocking albums on the Canadian Attic label.

A bit wiser this time, the Zazulas' started plastering telephone poles with flyers for their second concert. It would feature Anvil, Raven and Riot. Jonny Z (as he was called) says that Raven were "like gods to us." Signees to the NWOBHM's premier Neat label, Raven was originally from the British coal town of Newcastle. Riot was a New York hard-rock five-piece, around since the mid-seventies, that tended to have greater success touring Europe than the States.

The Anvil-Raven-Riot show drew 2,700 people to the St. George on New York's Staten Island. As befitted a place called the St. George, the Zazulas had built a fire-breathing dragon in the lobby, and even held an S and M bondage suit contest. Referring to New York's most powerful concert promoter, Jon Zazula recalls, "Even Jon Scher was catching wind of it."

Soon, the Zazulas were promoting more shows, now at Brooklyn clubs such as L'Amour and the Brooklyn Zoo—which had previously ignored metal in favor of cover or tribute bands.

"All of a sudden, we created a whole entire scene throughout this area that started to expand," Jon explains. "Even L.A. had not developed in the way that we had this market going over here. They maybe had local bands—maybe Mötley Crüe were kids then—but it wasn't bringing Europe to America."

One afternoon, a young metal fan walked into Rock N' Roll Heaven with Metallica's *No Life 'Til Leather* demo. Telling Jon and Marsha that the tape was phenomenal, he asked them to play it in the store. Jon and Marsha had no policy of playing demos, but they popped the cassette into the deck nonetheless. What they heard struck them as utterly wild and original—an American metal that was in their opinion an improvement on the NWOBHM. Whoever this fan was, he was right—this was a helluva band.

Through Ron Quintana, then a deejay at San Francisco radio station KUSF, Metallica was located. Jonny Z, in his enthusiasm, talked about managing the band, and maybe even making a record—things, like retailing and concert promotion, that he'd never done before. (But Jon and Marsha Zazula were proving themselves pretty quick studies.) Fortunately, the Zazulas had set up a dozen or so dates for British proto-thrashers Venom and domestic metalheads the Rods. Metallica was invited to join the bill.

The Zazulas' combination of management, concerts and recording was the best offer Metallica had ever seen. James, Lars, Cliff and Dave would make the cross-country trek to the Zazulas' home in Old Bridge, New Jersey.

When the Metallica vehicle pulled up in front of the Zazula house, Jon and Marsha were at the record store, as usual. When they finally met Metallica, they weren't fully aware of the fact that this band that had driven three thousand miles to meet them was just about dead broke. Although still enthusiastic, the Zazulas were starting to wonder just what the hell it was they were getting themselves into.

Metallica's home in the New York metropolitan area was in the Music Building in Yonkers, north of New York City. Like all other Music Buildings in all other cities, this was the only rehearsal space available for musicians who live in garage-free areas. Such places tend to be filled to the rafters with harried future superstars—each trying to shove two guitars, a mike stand, a bass drum and three Marshall amps into one tiny elevator. Landlords usually advised bands not to try to live in a Music Building, but there were always a few, like Metallica, who did.

Metallica shared its rehearsal space with another young metal band, Anthrax. Since Metallica had no money and no way of cooking and storing food, the guys in Anthrax scrounged an oven and a refrigerator for them. Like some sort of heavy metal relief agency, Anthrax would sometimes bring the hungry Metallicans, who were living on little more than baloney sandwiches, a little food as well.

Anthrax started out as a part of New York's hardcore scene, but soon caught the new metal bug and proceeded to write their own distinctly punkish book on thrash-metal with irreverent wit and a maniacal, mosh-inspiring mayhem.

Ultimately to become New York's greatest contribution to the new metal scene, the original members of Anthrax were lead singer Neil Turbin, guitarist Scott Ian, a guitarist recruited from Over Kill named Dan Spitz, bassist Dan Lilker and drummer Charlie Benante. Their producer in the early days was Ross the Boss from Manowar. (An Anthrax gig with Manowar got Ross interested.) Jon and Marsha Zazula started managing the band in 1983.

Before too long, Turbin and Lilker left the band—Lilker to form radioactive thrashers Nuclear Assault. They were replaced by singer Joey Belladonna and bassist Frank Bello.

Now, with the cooking apparatus supplied by Anthrax, the Metallica crew could eat burgers with Hamburger Helper while they scarfed down low-cost Schlitz Malt Liquor.

Although Jon Zazula felt for the band in their reduced

circumstances, he still wasn't sure he wanted them in his home. Ultimately, the band's living conditions at the Music Building became so hard that the Zazulas let the band move in with them.

Unfortunately, Raven were also staying with Jon and Marsha at the time. Sometimes Venom were guests. In fact, lots of bands stayed with Jon and Marsha at what came to be known as Megaforce Castle. In its sheer population density of rock musicians, the Zazulas' home tended to resemble the big hippie band-houses of late sixties San Francisco. The place always seemed crowded and the lawn was littered with empty bottles of beer or the licorice-schnapps concoction Jägermeister. The township of Old Bridge actually sent Jon and Marsha letters disapproving of their strange-looking guests. (The official warning was later included as a part of the artwork for the *Megavault* album.) Ultimately, the Zazulas grew weary of being the proprietors of a heavy metal motel. They both worked during the day, and were raising two children to boot. And it could be a little unnerving having to entrust all their worldly possessions with whomever happened to be living there at the time. Still, Metallica stayed with the Zazulas for quite a while.

As Metallica's new manager, Jon had tried to interest major labels in the *No Life 'Til Leather* demos. Arista Records and, amusingly enough, Elektra Records both heard the tape and were unimpressed. Jon's stock suggestion was that they weren't listening to the cash registers if they couldn't understand the music. But the major labels heard neither.

Calling Metallica the new Led Zeppelin, Jon Zazula turned publicist, creating interest in the band even without a record deal.

Finally, after failing to attract a record company, Jon and Marsha decided to record the album themselves. But

Jon Zazula had a fairly low opinion of some metal labels, which he felt were putting out little more than demos on vinyl. If Jon and Marsha were going to run a label, they wanted to put some polish on their releases.

With the first release for Megaforce Records (later Megaforce Worldwide) now in the planning stage, the Zazulas had a number of irons in the fire. Their new management company, Crazed Management, was representing Raven; Manowar wanted to work with them; and the Anthraxers, fixtures at all the Zazula-promoted shows, would later join the Crazed crew. And Rock N' Roll Heaven was doing better then ever.

When Megaforce Worldwide had become an established label, Marsha Zazula told *Billboard,* "You won't find Megaforce signing guys who look like women playing crap. We have to work. We sign the underdog. The idea is to sell three million records while keeping your integrity."

In 1984, Megaforce would release Anthrax's debut album, *Fistful of Metal.* Every subsequent Anthrax album has been recorded for Megaforce Worldwide and distributed by Island Records. In 1986, with the demands of a music empire on their hands, Jon and Marsha Zazula closed Rock N' Roll Heaven.

Other signees to Megaforce have been King's X, Frehleys Comet, M.O.D. (Method of Destruction), Testament, Over Kill and the progressive-metal band Prophet.

But for now, the Zazulas' job was cut out for them: to get that wild-riffing, adrenaline-enhancing Metallica sound onto vinyl.

5

In 1983, Metallica seemed to be getting everything right. They had a real—if only nascent—management and record label, and the tour dates were starting to roll in. But more touring had accented another problem: Dave Mustaine.

Band members that are the best of friends at home have been known to bicker violently under the amplified pressures of the road. And Dave's fights with the band were becoming legendary—as was his substance abuse. Whether the problem was indeed booze or drugs or just simply strong, incompatible personalities, it was becoming clearer every day that Dave's negative qualities were outweighing his positive ones.

Musically, Dave's course was diverging from that of the rest of the band. He played the speediest guitar parts with his customary flair, and his rhythm playing was acceptable, but when the band strayed over into more melodic neighborhoods, Dave tended to lose his way. From Dave's perspective, there were too many creative cooks elbowing each other for space in one cramped, hard-rocking kitchen.

"James and Lars were really focused in their own way, and I wasn't," Dave recalled years later to *Music Connection*. "I begged to differ with almost everything just for the sake of being argumentative."

Dave also recalled an incident that he says precipitated his split. At some drunken gathering or other, James Hetfield allegedly kicked Dave's dog. Defending the honor of his pooch, Dave punched James. The ensuing fight, according to Dave, ended in—well, either Dave's firing or his resignation, depending on one's viewpoint.

Metallica's New York soundman, intimately aware of the band's turmoil, told them of the guitar player for a San Francisco band called Exodus. After hearing some tapes of Exodus, the Metallicans found themselves singularly impressed with the guitarist, Kirk Hammett. In eleventh-hour desperation before recording the album that would become *Kill 'Em All*, Metallica asked Kirk to come out to New York. Luckily, he did.

Kirk Hammett was born on November 18, 1962. His father was a salesman and his mother worked for the federal government. Growing up in the San Francisco suburb of El Sobrante, Kirk's first-ever record album was *The Partridge Family Christmas*.

Kirk's earliest memory of childhood is letting his brother's bicycle roll down three flights of stairs. Like David Hetfield, Kirk's big brother played a crucial role in Kirk's career destiny. Kirk's brother could have also been described as a hippie, and had been playing guitar since the late sixties on San Francisco's Haight-Ashbury scene. Kirk found himself drawn into the electrified worlds of Santana, Jimi Hendrix (especially *Band of Gypsies*) and Led Zeppelin (especially *Physical Graffitti*). Without any fraternal influence,

Kirk and his friends enjoyed the theatrical pop-metal of Kiss—Kirk even dressed up like Kiss lead guitarist Ace Frehley one Halloween. Kirk's tastes became a bit more refined as he got older, leaning toward progressive East Coast punks Minor Threat, the horror-core band the Misfits, and British agit-punk legends Discharge. Aside from the ubiquitous Hendrix, the virtuosic Michael Schenker ranked high among Kirk's personal guitar gods.

Kirk's first *real* band was formed in 1981. A five-piece called Legend, his bandmates included vocalist Paul Baloff, guitarist Gary Holt, bassist Jeff Andrews and drummer Tom Hunting. Before long, Legend had changed its name to Exodus. The band gigged around the Bay Area, hitting such rock joints as the Stone in San Francisco and the Omni in Oakland. In 1982, Exodus released their *Bonded by Blood* album, which evoked favorable comparisons to Slayer.

One of Kirk's old friends—they met in high school algebra class—was Les Claypool, later of Primus. With Kirk in Exodus and Les in Blind Illusion, the two always found themselves running with the same local-band crowd. As a player, Les never forgot Kirk's verve—or his leopard-print clothes. Primus would continue, with vocalist and lyricist Claypool, as the definitive funk-metal hybrid.

When Kirk left Exodus for Metallica, he was replaced by Rick Hunolt. Exodus also added wailing frontman Steve Souza, formerly of another local act called Legacy. Legacy would later change its name to Testament and, through a series of hard'n'fast Megaforce albums, go on to national fame for their bracing speedmetal.

With Gary Holt the only original Legend member left, Exodus raged on into nineties on the Relativity label, never swerving from its maniacal, mondo-metal stance. A well-known Exodus sweatshirt once proclaimed: "FOUR ALBUMS AND STILL NO BALLAD."

With money borrowed from his mother, Kirk Hammett packed up his guitar and flew to New York. Kirk's flight would land in the afternoon. Earlier that same day, Dave Mustaine had left.

Despite a sense of if-this-doesn't-work-out-what-do-we-do-then, James, Lars and Cliff plugged in to rehearse with Kirk. From Kirk's first blistering solo on "Seek and Destroy," the band was positive that they'd made the right choice.

From Kirk's first gig with Metallica at the Showplace in Dover, New Jersey (supported by Anthrax), he felt that Metallica was actually better suited to his personal playing style than Exodus had been. For Lars, Kirk's guitar solos had what he'd so often sought, a European sound. Kirk believed that this was because of his use of harmonic minor scales—which can give off a Middle Eastern aura. Artists like Ritchie Blackmore were pioneers of the sound, while latter-day guitar heroes like Yngwie Malmsteen would nearly perfect it.

The cut-loose Dave Mustaine's first act as an ex-Metallican was to fashion his own brand of speedmetal—which was starting to be called "thrash," for whatever reasons. Dave remembered an antinuclear brochure from California senator Alan Cranston that warned of the millions of deaths (megadeaths) that would result from a thermonuclear war. With the loss of one vowel, Dave's new band had its name.

Mustaine released Megadeth's Combat Records debut album *Killing Is My Business ... and Business Is Good* in 1985. *Killing* contained one song that Metallica used to play, albeit briefly: "Mechanix," which could be called the birth of Megadeth. The Metallica version began with a lovely, halting, baroque-sounding theme on bass and piano. A hypnotic speedriff swallows it up as the howled vocals rise above the jagged accompaniment.

Megadeth's original members were Chris Poland on guitar, Dave "Junior" Ellefson on bass and Gary Samuelson on drums. Kerry King from Slayer was also briefly in the band. Megadeth was soon picked up by Capitol Records, which distributed its subsequent Combat albums.

Mustaine remains unsurpassed in his nonstop attacks on the ills of society and entrenched authoritarianism, from *Peace Sells . . . but Who's Buying?*, an album that probes the amorality of international war-merchants, to such songs as "Hangar 18," which speak of a government cover-up on a cosmic scale. Megadeth's brilliantly inspired, unforgettable album covers depict ruthless, death-headed men of the military-industrial complex. Over the years, these illustrations have offered a harsh visual representation of the fears of society's powerless.

In the years immediately following his parting with Metallica, Dave Mustaine wasted no chances attacking the band for any number of reasons: they didn't credit him for songs he'd cowritten, they weren't playing hard and fast enough anymore—the list goes on. Dave also sought to deride Jon Zazula and Megaforce while he was at it.

In interviews, Dave pumped up the apocryphal story that it was he who came up with the band's name—a neat trick, considering that Lloyd Grant was still the band's guitarist when the name was found. Dave also reinforced the false rumor that the name "Metallica" was a combination of the words "metal" and "vodka."

"It was weird for a while. There was a lot of weird things going on in the press between us and Mustaine for a couple of years," Lars told MTV years after the split. "I think that it was just that Dave was kind of bitter. It wasn't like the sweetest of breakups."

In the same MTV interview show, Kirk Hammett told of meeting Dave Mustaine years after Mustaine had left Metallica: "It was really unusual because I was standing there and I'm always polite about it—'Hi Dave, hiya doin'?' And he goes, 'Hey, hiya doin'?' And basically he just came up to me and apologized for all the bad-mouthing that he did to me and the band. I was really surprised. I think that was a result of him cleaning up and actually being able to think with a clear head . . . I thought it was very decent of him."

Calling his tenure with Metallica "magical yet impossible," Dave Mustaine also told *Music Connection*, "I was the guitar player in Metallica, Hetfield was the mastermind behind the lyrics and Lars was back there banging on his drum set. We gave this style of music a format and a direction—I'll always be proud of that."

By the end of the eighties, Megadeth had undergone several personnel changes and some much-needed (rock) group therapy. Dave succeeded in exorcising his personal demons, and under his guidance, Megadeth's elaborate, dazzling riffery continued into the nineties.

6

> **There is an obvious similarity between speed/thrash's challenge to heavy metal and the contestation, initiated by Martin Luther and John Calvin, against the Catholic Church.**
>
> —**Deena Weinstein,** *Heavy Metal*

In May of 1983, James Hetfield, Lars Ulrich, Cliff Burton and the freshly hired Kirk Hammett drove north to Music America studios in Rochester, New York. Sending the band to Rochester was a better investment for Jonny Z than watching the dollars tick by at some pricey Manhattan studio. Around four weeks in production, the debut Metallica album cost only $12,000 to make—but it was a small fortune to the newly arrived Zazulas. Paul Curcio is listed as the producer for the album, although band recollections indicate that, by and large, he left them to their own devices.

The seven songs written before the *No Life 'Til Leather* demo were re-recorded at Music America, with expanded versions of "Jump in the Fire," "Phantom Lord," "Seek and Destroy" and "Metal Militia," whose anthemic qualities are further outlined by a finale of marching feet and the sounds of war.

Most drastically changed was "The Four Horsemen," reworked to feature a beautiful middle section that echoes

Cliff's intense bassmanship put him in the spotlight.
Courtesy Kevin Hodapp.

the classic chords of "Sweet Home Alabama," by one of James's favorites, Lynyrd Skynyrd.

"Whiplash," appearing for the first time on the album, is a bone-crushing call to party—a thrash anthem whose tempo and riffing are emblematic of the newborn movement. Years of hindsight led James embarrassedly to tell *Musician* that much of their earliest lyrics were "really kind of Judas Priest, '*Let's go rock out . . .'* "

Despite any less-than-thoughtful words that may have found their way onto the album, Metallica was crossing frontiers. Traditional metal, from Led Zep through Saxon, had been based on the blues. The new metal Metallica was shaping was built on the harder, more angular harmonies of punk. James and Lars's writing would often employ chords that lurch up at half-step intervals—a sound more akin to horror movie soundtracks than the blues. James has referred to the half-step approach as more "evil." Maybe it wasn't exactly a Rock Reformation, but there was *some* kind of metal revolution going on there.

A dark vision of conflict eternal, "No Remorse" also made its recorded debut at Music America. The song's chugging, Motörheadish riff takes an abrupt shift into a loping, near-raga beat—what might be considered a moshing cue for bands to come. Adorned with distinct parts and rhythm changes, "No Remorse" is the kind of Metallica theme that could've been included on . . . *And Justice for All*, recorded five years later.

Metallica couldn't record an album without paying homage to Cliff Burton's sterling bassmanship. "(Anesthesia) Pulling Teeth" begins with a rhapsodic, Rachmaninoffian melody line, followed by Cliff offering the listener a rare vision of funk-rock meeting English madrigals—adorned by his delicious, nimble-fingered embellishments.

* * *

The working title for Metallica's debut album was *Metal Up Your Ass*. Indelicate, but the band no doubt felt it got the point across. When the prospective album distributor's people heard the title, they promptly informed Jonny Z that he'd better start looking for a new distributor. But the band was adamant.

A compromise idea was floated that they go acronymic, calling the album *M.U.Y.A.*, but the band wasn't having it. Ultimately, Jon Zazula trekked up to Rochester to tell the band that their music needed to be given a chance—and it didn't need a title that would close doors for them. After a few forget-it-that-one-sucks reactions to possible new album titles, Cliff Burton's exasperation at the record distributors could contain itself no longer. "Kill 'em all, man," he exclaimed. "Just kill 'em all." It was the only title that worked.

Kill 'Em All was released in 1983 emblazoned with the Hetfield-designed, fish-hooked Metallica logo. The album's liner notes allow the band to thank the usual assortment of friends, other bands and writers, as well as their road crew—a group seldom noted except possibly on live albums. Also graciously thanked are former bandmates Dave Mustaine and Ron McGovney, as well as the members of Exodus and Trauma. (They also manage to get a quick "Metal Up Your Ass" in there for good measure.) Most interesting is the section of the liner notes that issues nonthanks—actually "HUGE AMOUNTS OF HATRED AND CESS RIDDEN FILTH"—to a number of unhelpful people, places and companies.

Kill 'Em All sold twenty thousand copies in its first two weeks of release—an incredible feat for a first-time independent album.

* * *

Under the aegis of Jonny Z, Metallica's first national jaunt involved opening up for Raven, on what was billed as the Kill 'Em All for One tour—from a combination of the names of the two bands' Megaforce albums, *Kill 'Em All* and *All for One*. The two bands shared a crew and a Winnebago. John Ditmar, a booking agent the Zazulas had met at a Talas gig, made up the contracts and did the routing for the tour. These tours were by no means luxury equipped. The band was living in cramped quarters and the tour—while helping to create a loyal fan base—wasn't exactly making anybody rich. But the band did what they wanted to do—play. Backed by a simple black-and-white cloth "Metallica" banner, James was already refining his audience-participation call-and-response chant of their somewhat unorthodox rallying cry: "Metal Up Your Ass!"

Everything fell into place: James downstroked his white Flying V viciously, Kirk soloed with flash-fingered abandon, Cliff's Rickenbacker sang with eloquent rumblings and Lars logo-bedecked bass drums punctuated the enveloping racket. (When the tour was in Chicago, Jon and Marsha flew out to meet the band for a less-than-successful attempt to shoot a music video.)

On the Midwest leg of the Kill 'Em All for One tour, the local promoter had convinced somebody to put on six shows at huge, amphitheater-sized venues. (With the prospect of selling no more than a few hundred tickets to any of these shows, smaller rock clubs would've been the right size.) When the bands arrived at one giant hall— where only about 150 tickets had been sold—the facility representatives wanted to know if the bands had any lighting or pyrotechnics that needed to be rigged up. Naturally, a low-budget club tour such as this would have none. But then, neither did some of these huge amphitheaters. At one of these ludicrous arena shows in Oklahoma, the crew had to approach local farmers to borrow fork lifts. The borrowed fork lifts were used to hold up the band's borrowed lighting before a cavernous, nearly empty hall. Despite some problems in the hinterlands, Metallica's return to San Francisco was nothing short of triumphant.

7

> The Thing of the idols, the green, sticky spawn of the stars, had awaked to claim his own. The stars were right again, and what an age-old cult had failed to do by design, a band of innocent sailors had done by accident. After vigintillions of years great Cthulhu was loose again, and ravening for delight.
>
> —H. P. Lovecraft,
> *The Call of Cthulhu*

"We had a record out, we were touring, but we really couldn't play," was how Lars described to *Spin* the band's realization that they were playing in the big leagues. They started to clean up their musical acts somewhat. Lars started taking drum lessons and Kirk started studying under the Berkeley-based rock guitar virtuoso Joe Satriani. Kirk said that his study with Satriani expanded and freed up his perspective on the guitar, allowing him to play anywhere on the neck in any key instead of seeing the guitar neck as a series of isolated positions.

Marsha Zazula designed the first Metallica tour T-shirts—"KILL 'EM ALL FOR ONE" and "METAL UP YOUR ASS." Still often seen even ten years after its creation, the dagger-clenching-fist-in-a-toilet-bowl of "METAL UP YOUR ASS" has joined the popular iconography of heavy metal, along with

Motörhead's tusked war helmets and Iron Maiden's walking-dead Eddie.

The touring, as ever, was austere. The band's per diem, their daily allotment of money, was said to have been $5 per member. Despite the most creative low-budgetry the Zazulas could manage, the business was putting them into debt—there was a very good reason Jon became known for the phrase "the well is dry."

Except for all the requisite alcohol consumption, there was something about early Metallica tours that resembled summer camp. "We used to sleep four to a room. I had to share a bed with Lars," Kirk recalled to *Creem Metal.* "He used to take all the blankets. I would never sleep with Cliff, because he had really pointed elbows. Really bony. Actually, no one snores much. We drool a lot."

There were, of course, good reasons to settle for less-than-deluxe accommodations. Metallica's six-day European jaunt with Venom, during which they stayed in uncharacteristically fine hotels, ended up costing over $35,000.

In the spring of 1984, Lars Ulrich returned to his childhood home of Copenhagen, Denmark, to record Metallica's second album *Ride the Lightning.* Album production was credited to Lars, James, Cliff and Kirk, with Flemming Rasmussen and Mark Whitaker.

As Lars told British radio at the time: "We're in the process of recording our second album at Sweet Silence studios in Copenhagen, where Rainbow have recorded a couple of albums. The album productionwise is a total step forward from *Kill 'Em All.* It's got really, really huge drum sounds and it sounds really, really professional. We're experimenting with things at a little slower pace now. We feel that you're kinda limited if you only play fast all the time. It's great, especially onstage, playing fast, but there's very few things for variations you can do when the tempo's up that fast."

The best evidence of Metallica's interest in slower, more acoustically oriented songs came with "Fade to Black." A relentless, seemingly bottomless plunge into the depression that beckons suicide, "Fade to Black" begins with an exquisitely lonely guitar aria played before a sympathetic chorus of glistening acoustics. Its beautiful vocal line weaves back and forth like a man on a window ledge, staring out over the abyss.

The critics of metal would see an endorsement of suicide in the first-person narration of "Fade to Black." However, Metallica fan club chief K. J. Doughton told *The New York Times* that the song brought a huge written response from Metallica's growing legions of female fans (something of an anomaly in male-oriented metal). Their letters were extremely positive—the song's suicide theme steering them farther away from such an act, rather than encouraging them towards it.

In fact, the inspiration for "Fade to Black" may have been less grandiose than suicidal depression. It has been suggested that the song reflects the band's shock and despondency after they'd had their equipment stolen shortly before they left to record *Ride the Lightning*.

"Escape" is a fierce depiction of the individual's struggle against domination. Despite its overshadowing guitar riff, the song actually has—Heaven forbid!—a pop-oriented vocal hook.

The horror and the scorched moral grounds of war are painted with broad strokes in "For Whom the Bell Tolls," a song whose riffs move ravenously, like barbarian armies swarming across the tundra. As the song ends, an ominous clock tower chimes away heedlessly while guitars wail in the mix like lost souls in the underworld.

"Ride the Lightning" is a bleak assessment of the death penalty, as seen through the eyes of a condemned man. An older song (cowritten with Dave Mustaine), it's propelled by a fat, belching riff with twin guitars that swirl into upper-register curlicues of sound. James's mad-monk-on-the-heath vocals and dramatic multitracked voices add to the song's horror-movie ambience.

It can be said that the success of *Kill 'Em All* actually helped create songs like "Ride the Lightning." After the band had some money coming in from *Kill 'Em All* and their subsequent touring, Lars and James scraped together enough cash to buy a television set. They were immediately drawn to the TV news and the social issues that it detailed. Songs like "Ride the Lightning" showed the influence of TV news on their songwriting.

"Fight Fire with Fire" is a prophecy of atomic apocalypse, a topic frequently on the minds of people living under the renewed nuclear brinksmanship of the Reagan years. It begins with a lovely acoustic court-dance, which is immediately plowed through by a locomotive guitar riff, although the guitars do return for a light, stylish fantasia. On these *Lightning* sessions, James's voice has very nearly become the one he would sing with throughout his career—more oomph and less shriek.

A biblical vision of remorseless retribution, "Creeping Death" conjures up Viking-movie dramatics with its slave-ship chants of "Die ...!" "Die ...!" thereafter became a particular favorite line for fans to join in on at shows—although when they chant it outside the venue, it has been known to make bystanders uneasy.

An older instrumental theme, "The Call of Ktulu" is a sound-alike title of Lovecraft's story of an all-powerful dormant god given an inadvertent wake-up call. Led by Cliff

Burton's bass, its tense, dreamlike guitar pickings are transformed by powerful, cinematic riffs into an atmosphere of menaced panic.

Ride the Lightning, the production cost of which approached $50,000, was released in 1984 on Megaforce Records. Its liner notes contained an even larger thank-you section than did those of *Kill 'Em all,* this time divided among friends on the East Coast, West Coast and Europe. Making his first appearance in this section was K. J. Doughton, who ran the Oregon-based fan club (the address of which was listed on the album jacket). And, obviously still not quite recovered from the indignity of changing their first album's title, Metallica put "Metal Up Your Ass" in there a second time.

During the production of *Ride the Lightning,* a short British tour was planned for Metallica, Exciter and the Rods, by the Music for Nations group in England. Unfortunately, poor ticket sales quashed the idea. In the U.K. with no tour, Lars spoke to the BBC: "It's a pity about the economical situation here when kids only have enough money to go to shows once a month or twice a month," Lars commented. "Of course they'll choose the bands that they're familiar with— a band like Whitesnake—so they know they'll get value for their money." Although they could draw tickets away from harder metal acts in 1984, Whitesnake (led by ex–Deep Purple vocalist David Coverdale) would ultimately fall victim to its own success and suffer from a universal I-never-liked-those-guys fan backlash.

At the time of *Ride the Lightning,* Metallica was starting to release European twelve-inch EPs through their British label Vertigo. In early 1984, Vertigo released a twelve-inch of

"Jump in the Fire" with a flame-bathed, Lovecraftian demon adorning the cover. The flip side contained live versions of "Seek and Destroy" and "Phantom Lord."

Later that year, Vertigo released a twelve-inch EP version of "Creeping Death." The B side of "Creeping Death" consisted of two NWOBHM cover tunes. "Blitzkrieg" is a straightforward 1981 metal tune by a band of the same name from the British city of Leicester. More significant is the inclusion of Diamond Head's 1980 occult-themed rocker "Am I Evil?," driven by a punchy, lurching riff. Nearly eight minutes in length, "Am I Evil?" is clearly a song Metallica wishes *it* had written. "Am I Evil" has been a concert staple ever since.

As usual, Metallica was bashing away at their music or trashing away at their recreational activities, when other people in other places had plans for them.

One was Michael Alago, a young new-music fan who booked the New York rock club the Ritz. The Ritz tended towards the alternative scene, and to it Alago brought such punk stalwarts as the Dead Kennedys, the Misfits, the Undead, the False Prophets and the Birthday Party.

With only his experience in club booking behind him, Michael Alago was hired to be an A&R representative for Elektra Records in 1983. (A&R, originally "artists and repertoire," is the department that brings new talent to a label.) Alago had no track record to speak of, but when Elektra chairman Bob Krasnow hired Alago, he had an intuitive sense that Alago was right for the job.

"Somebody had played me *Kill 'Em All,* and I freaked out," recalls Michael Alago. "You have to remember that when that record came out in the beginning of '83, I had just gotten to Elektra, and bands like Slayer and Megadeth or any of the bands we know today as thrash or new-metal/

speedmetal bands were all nonexistent. People were still listening to the staples: Ozzy, Judas Priest, Iron Maiden. . . ." Alago was so taken with *Kill 'Em All* that it spent most of 1983 on his turntable. Alago was aware that the band was signed to the Zazulas' independent Megaforce label, but thought it might be approachable with a good deal. Still new at Elektra, Alago wasn't sure how to convince his higher-ups that thrash-metal belonged on a major record label. Although Alago was new at A&R, he was aware of the A&R man's nightmare—to sign a group that costs the label a fortune only to "stiff."

In time, though, Michael Alago would grow bolder. "The beginning of '84 rolls around and I found Lars in San Francisco. I called him and told him that I was absolutely mad about his band and that I had to sign them," Alago recalls. "He said, 'The next time we're coming around it's part of a package deal with Anthrax and Raven and we're in the middle. When we come to New York, we'll call you.' " Although Alago had been interested in some demos that Raven had been working on, he soon lost all interest in anything but Metallica.

The show that Lars told Michael to catch was at New York's famed dance hall Roseland, which has never been averse to add slamming to its ballroom and disco events. Alago got a ticket for the Raven-Metallica-Anthrax show. He also got tickets for label chief Bob Krasnow and Mike Bone, then Elektra's senior VP of promotion and marketing. Michael Alago was enthusiastic enough to bring the big honchos to the Metallica show. In fact, Alago was so enthusiastic, he'd never even seen Metallica *once* before in his life. This was Alago's first big A&R decision, and he seemed to be betting the farm. "I don't know," Alago remembers of the night, "I just kind of lost my mind . . . because the record was so staggering and the press and things I'd read about them were so wonderful that I thought: 'All these people can't be wrong.' "

Although Mike Bone wasn't quite sure of what he was hearing, he did what any practical music-business executive would do—he checked out the T-shirt concession. The Metallica shirts were already sold out.

Michael Alago remembers: "The minute the show was over, I don't even think I had a backstage pass but I just made my way to the back and I said, 'All of you are not to go *anywhere* but my office tomorrow.'

"And here I was this drunk, crazy person, I must have been twenty-two years old or something," Alago continues. "They were like 'Are you for real?' And I said, 'Yes, I do A&R at Elektra and we're the only place you should come.' And Cliff, bless his soul, said, 'Is there gonna be lots of beer there?' And I said, 'Whatever you want. I'll order Chinese and you'll come.' "

By noon the following day, the sleepy-eyed members of Metallica filed into Michael Alago's midtown Manhattan office. "They all crammed into my little office at Elektra. There was tons of Chinese food and beer there," Alago recalls, "They played me bits and pieces of *Ride the Lightning* and I had my Polaroid camera and I was taking Polaroids and sticking them up on the walls of my office. We just got along like a house on fire, all of us."

Now more positive than ever that Metallica belonged on Elektra Records, Alago told the band "that this record they were making sounded too important to be put out on an independent label." Alago sensed that another major label would snatch up the band if he didn't act soon—he was determined to make Metallica the first "thrash" band to be signed to a major record label.

Alago's enthusiasm paid off. "They liked me because

I was very young and enthusiastic and was totally nuts about them, was willing to die for them," he recalls. "So it just kind of worked out perfectly and I think they really liked the history of Elektra because they knew about all the records that had come out on Elektra in the sixties and seventies." As well as signing offbeat folkies like Tim Buckley, Jackson Browne and Joni Mitchell, Elektra was home to such rock icons as the Doors, the Stooges with Iggy Pop, the MC5 and Queen.

Michael Alago then approached Jon Zazula about signing the band to Elektra. "After my meeting with the Metallica boys I said to Jon, 'You know, I've met with the boys in the band and you can't put this record out on an independent label, it sounds too important.' "

Metallica was signed to a long-term recording agreement with Elektra Records late in 1984. *Ride the Lightning,* which was originally released as a Megaforce album in the fall of 1984, would later appear with both companies' logos on the back. Elektra even created a sixty-second radio ad for *Ride the Lightning.* Narrated by the distinctively deep-toned New York radio veteran Scott Muni, it featured snippets from "For Whom the Bell Tolls" and "Fade to Black." Muni's resonant voice beckoned, "Maybe you think you've heard metal. Well it's high time you heard the *real thing.* It's time you heard *Metallica.*"

Megaforce had done very well for the band that started off as a demo in the tape deck at Rock N' Roll Heaven. As a testament to Jon Zazula's abilities as a press agent, one top Elektra executive said that Megaforce–Crazed Management had done at least a two-million-dollar promo job on Metallica to get them to where they were. Naturally, Jon "The Well Is Dry" Zazula had managed the task for a lot less.

*　*　*

Of course, not everyone at Elektra was positive that Michael Alago's signing of Metallica was such a brilliant idea. Elektra honcho Bob Krasnow—who probably didn't want to be reminded of the band's Roseland gig—was not interested in hearing the band around the office, despite Michael Alago's enthusiasm. "He indulged me," Alago remembers. "He allowed me to just do what I wanted to there. It worked out well."

After finding and signing artists to a record label, the A&R rep's next duty is often in the "development" of the band. The A&R man would keep an eye on their songwriting, see that their creative needs were met, and in general guide the band towards making better music. Metallica, however, has never been known as a band that took outside suggestions very well. Or at all.

"They were so focused it was kind of easy on my end," Michael recollects of working with the band. "It was just a matter of being really encouraging to them and always being around when they needed me."

On a personal basis, Alago and the band got along swimmingly, for the most part. "James and I, in the beginning, kind of didn't get along because we were definitely two different types of people," Michael remembers. "Then at some party in San Francisco, with both of our heads in a toilet bowl, we kind of bonded. After that, we got along famously, him and I. But it took a very long time because we're definitely two different types of people."

Metallica's Roseland gig held even more for them than a major label deal. Representatives from the major management firm Q Prime were there as well. "The ball was rolling. A lot of people then were talking about them and there was interest," Alago recalls. "When they got signed to Elektra, they wound up signing with Q Prime also."

Q Prime saw the potential in a band that seemed to have as wide an underground following as Metallica. "When I went to that Roseland gig," Cliff Burnstein told *Billboard*, "I felt old for the first time. There was a whole new breed of fans."

With some negotiations, Q Prime bought Metallica's management contract from Crazed Management. The ties between Metallica and the Zazulas were then, for all practical purposes, broken. For independent entrepreneurs like the Zazulas to have big-money label and management move in on a band they had done so much to nurture—and let live in their house—resentment would be natural. Still, Jonny and Marsha Z returned to their growing Megaforce Worldwide–Crazed Management empire and wished Metallica well.

Q Prime management always prided itself on overseeing all aspects of an artist's career—the touring, the recording, the releasing of singles, the radio exposure, the video exposure, and so forth. In addition to Metallica, Q Prime artists past and present have included Queensrÿche, Def Leppard, Tesla, Suicidal Tendencies, Warrior Soul, Armored Saint, White Trash, the Dan Reed Network, AC/DC, Dokken and the Scorpions.

Q Prime's Cliff Burnstein is a rarity in the world of music management—it has been written that he makes all his calls himself, without secretarial intervention.

Q Prime, like Elektra Records, felt Metallica was best left alone to make music in their own style. Cliff Burnstein has been quoted as saying that Q Prime didn't sign acts if the company didn't already like the way they were.

Lars has stated that Q Prime felt European audiences would be more receptive to Metallica—so Europe was where Q Prime concentrated its energies. The band was smart enough not to want overnight success, knowing that longest careers are developed slowly and carefully. It would have been a psychological death knell, Lars thought, if Metallica had become the accursed Next Big Thing.

Another aspect of the Q Prime plan was for Metallica to play in as many venues as possible. "That's great because it's the classic way to do things," Lars remarked to *Circus*. "Just tour and tour and build it up from the bottom. Fuck the radio and video and all that shit."

Metallica, no strangers to the road, were about to develop a much closer relationship. "I think we played some of our best music in those days and in those places," Lars later recalled to *Hit Parader* of their early tours. "There was a kind of simple, straightforward purity to those shows that you just can't capture in a recording studio, no matter how hard you try."

With a reputation for boozemongering that was earning the band the nickname "Alcoholica," the band played some of Europe's biggest dates. They appeared at the German Metal Hammer Fest with Venom and long-lived Scottish hard-rockers Nazareth. With such Metallitunes as "Seek and Destroy" and "The Four Horsemen," the discerning German metal audience could hear for itself these Americans who were getting all this press.

The 1985 Castle Donington show was a turning point for the band. Although on a mostly speedmetal bill, the Metallica set featured such slower songs as "Fade to Black." Wary of conforming to any "movements," the band was already trying to shake off the thrash label—a label many feel they created.

Through mega–booking agency ICM, Q Prime was able to send Metallica on a very successful sixty-date tour with W.A.S.P. and Armored Saint that same year. The number of

Metallica fans was growing with every tour, and still more turned out for the sight of James howling through "Am I Evil?" or headbanger supremo Cliff Burton lashing the air with his hair. Burton in particular played to the crowd. With his riveting, wildly powerful bass style, Cliff sometimes needed to be reined in a bit during concerts, lest he overpower the band. But when it came to music, calls for restraint usually went unheeded by Cliff Burton.

Prior to the W.A.S.P. tour, Lars and James had been sharing a house which had a much-beloved practice space in its garage. While Lars and James were on tour, some of their "friends" did a less-than-stalwart job of keeping an eye on the place—lots of stuff just wasn't there anymore when they got back. For their next big tour, Lars and James remembered this lesson, and just plain moved out.

9

Unlike the first-songs effort of *Kill 'Em All* or the first-flush-of-freedom experimentation of *Ride the Lightning*, Metallica's third album would have to be a bit more mature. It would have to be a *premeditated* act of metal. And they were ready to further their break with lockstep thrash-metal. "We like playing fast, we like playing slow," Lars told *Creem*. "We like being melodic once in a while, we like being unmelodic, we like to throw a little bit of intelligence in there."

Almost more than knowing what to put into a song, Metallica was acutely aware of what *not* to put into a song. Tired or imitative metal bands stand like signposts to oblivion. "They have taught us how a band ought *not* to be," Lars remarked to *Melody Maker*. "You *can* be inspired by Poison, by realizing that you never, ever wanna be like *that*. That might sound stupid, but the more I think about it, the more I think that's what Metallica do. Because we're mostly *not* positively inspired by other bands, we spend more time consciously or unconsciously blocking out the things we dislike." The Reductive Method of Metallica: Whittle away anything that's stupid or boring, and whatever's left is Metallica.

Metallica spent the fall of 1985 back in Copenhagen at the now-familiar Sweet Silence studios. *Ride the Lightning* coproducer Flemming Rasmussen was once again behind the soundboard.

When the band recorded *Ride the Lightning,* Sweet Silence was the best studio they could use for the money they had to spend. For the third album, some band members thought, perhaps one of the studios back in the Bay Area would be more convenient. But when Metallica's hard-partying tendencies were taken into account, it was a fair guess that there would be too many hangers-on and hangers-out for the band to get much work done. They also considered recording in one of L.A.'s multitude of studios, but the band felt that the Los Angeles studio atmosphere could feel somewhat corporate—both in terms of the studio and the kinds of bands that rehearsed there. For a relaxing locale that allowed the band a chance to concentrate, Sweet Silence won the day.

One other benefit of Denmark in the late fall and early winter is the dispensing of what the Danish call "Christmas beer." Lars and James were frequent imbibers of Christmas beer while outside the soundproof sanctum of Sweet Silence. Lars once told *Creem* of the effect of too many Christmas beers on one of his bandmates: "James would start trying to talk Danish—completely pissed out of his face. . . . Good fun."

* * *

Master of Puppets refines the overtly political themes of *Ride the Lightning* into more subtle areas of manipulation, either personal or political.

The religious manipulations of a fund-raising Fundamentalist preacher are starkly caricatured in "Leper Messiah," a tough rocker accented by a spacy, falling-down-the-rabbit-hole riff.

The title track, "Master of Puppets," tells the story of drug addiction as a parable of power. Recognized as a new-metal masterpiece, the chorus of "Puppets" takes off on great black-winged riffs, then transforms itself into a poignant rhapsody of cascading guitars. (Old friends Anthrax inserted one quick sample of the word "MAS-TER" from "Master of Puppets" in their song "I'm the Man.")

There have been reports that the infamous Parents Music Resource Center had turned its censorious eye on "Master of Puppets" and found the song pro-drug. It would hardly be surprising for one of the PMRC's hypersensitive, literal-minded interpreters of rock lyrics to miss the obvious anti-drug message of the song. "For some reason, they listed the song 'Master of Puppets,' saying it was about getting kids to do drugs, or something," James told *Guitar Player*. "But they can find anything they want to find."

(The PMRC continues to keep files on many rock bands, one of which is Metallica. The lyrics to *every* song on *Master of Puppets* are kept on file at the PMRC, along with interviews, album reviews, concert reviews and other materials on the band.)

One of James's favorite riffs in the entire Metallica repertoire is that from "The Thing That Should Not Be," a riff that *Guitar Player* expert Joe Gore called "Cowboys from Hell." With a title that suggests the opinion of one of Lovecraft's refined characters regarding some horrible creature from the netherworld, "The Thing That Should Not Be" even contains a reference to a Lovecraftian dark god, a "great old one." Musically, it's an all-out thrash-throbber with chords that pile on top of each other with mounting tension.

"Battery," a full-tilt, metal berserker's over-the-edge assault, was written as an indirect tribute to San Francisco's Old Waldorf club, which was located on Battery Street.

The one song on *Master of Puppets* with the greatest cult appeal is "Welcome Home (Sanitarium)," a testament to defiance and self-affirmation in the face of crumbling sanity. Dramatic acoustic harmonies create another perfectly wrought dreamscape with a bittersweet vocal line caged by slowly spiraling guitars.

Album instrumental "Orion" is an elaborate, multipart work that features the soloing bass of Cliff Burton. In "Orion," the guitars rumble and chatter, then gain eloquence and begin to sing. A gong silences them, and Cliff ushers in the rolling bassline that underpins the plaintive, bluesy guitars. In "Orion," guitars testify like a trippy Greek chorus, then take up the waltz-time theme. (When Lars first heard this part of the song, he said it reminded him of a Swedish folksong.) As the song comes to a close, clog dancing gives way to monolithic chords and a savage solo. Attracted to the heartbreaking sonorities in the second half of "Orion," some radio programmers were said to have edited the over-eight-minute-long song down to something closer to three minutes.

The band felt that *Master of Puppets* was a breakthrough album. "We're doing things that a lot of other heavy metal bands have never touched on," Lars told *Spin*. "One of the reasons we've been able to is that we have a hundred percent freedom from our management and our record company. We're showing the industry that you can write eight-minute songs, you can be honest with yourself and

Megaforce chief Jon Zazula (crouching) rounds up Kirk, Lars, Cliff, and James for a quick snapshot.
Courtesy Kevin Hodapp.

your crowd, you don't have to put a huge, pretentious thing on."

Master of Puppets became the first Metallica album to receive admiring critical notices. Lars believed that its popularity had much to do with Metallica's unwillingness to fit nicely into the now-established "thrash" genre.

Except for the odd eviscerated version of "Orion," nothing from Master of Puppets got any commercial radio play. But then again, the senior VP of promotion and marketing for Elektra said he never even tried to get the album on the radio. As manager Cliff Burnstein told Billboard, "We didn't exactly accommodate radio with this album. There was fifty-five minutes of music on the record and only eight songs."

Both the label and management always harbored some dim hope that Metallica would be like those other bands and would actually record a song that would make it on to the radio or would even shoot a video that could get on MTV. Nonetheless, the band's creative control was absolute. If radio and videos weren't the Metallica way, Metallica would do without them.

Metallica's first tour in support of Master of Puppets was an opening spot for Ozzy Osbourne's cross-country Ultimate Tour in 1986.

After leaving Black Sabbath in 1979, Ozzy Osbourne had become the major metal act in the country, followed closely by Iron Maiden. His Blizzard of Ozz and Diary of a Madman albums quickly attained classic status. Signed to Jet Records in the U.K., Ozzy married the label head's daughter, Sharon Arden. As Sharon Osbourne, she would remain a central player in Ozzy's professional as well as personal life.

For Metallica, working every day with a genuine metal legend was already a thrill, but it was compounded when Ozzy told the band that Metallica reminded him of Black Sabbath in the early days. The band, label and management all felt that Ozzy and Sharon were owed a great debt of thanks for putting Metallica on their tour, exposing them to Ozzy's more mainstream metal audience.

Metallica's stage set consisted of three simple risers, upon which sat a smaller drum riser. Flanking the risers were three broad white crosses, replicating those on the cover of *Master of Puppets*. Similarly, the backdrop reflects the fiery warcolors of the album art.

Lars, drumsticks in hands, runs in place a little before hitting the stage, to wake up his muscles. It'll be the last chance Lars gets to hop around before burying himself in his drum kit. (Scarcely visible, Lars was dramatically lit when the strobe lights flashed on him in time with the final thrashing throes of "Creeping Death.")

The crowds screamed with approval when James and Kirk lined up their guitars for the slow, guitar-duet middle section of "Master of Puppets"—as they did when Kirk began his opening cadenza of "Am I Evil?" bathed in blue light. With a setlist that included such hard-hitting Metallica tunes as "Battery," "Damage, Inc.," "Seek and Destroy" and "For Whom the Bell Tolls," more and more concertgoers who came there to see Ozzy left the show fascinated by Metallica.

The tourbus, emblazoned with a mermaid along its full length, was the scene of the band's off-hours travel and video-watching. Aside from interminable press interviews, the band would also give record signings wherever the Elektra people could organize them. Drying out Magic

Marker after Magic Marker, the band autographed whatever the fans brought up, from albums to guitars to beer bottles to body parts.

One new development on the Ozzy tour was the appearance of the work of rock'n'roll artist Pushead, who was originally slated to draw a caricature of the band as a part of the *Master of Puppets* artwork. When the band went to Denmark to record the album, James left Pushead with the management company's phone number. Unfortunately, the number was wrong and Pushead never made contact. By the time the band came back from recording, it was too late to do any work for the album sleeve, but Pushead did design two T-shirts for this tour. They represented themes of "Damage, Inc." and the title of the Budgie song, "Crash Course in Brain Surgery." (Two Pushead-drawn caricatures ended up on Metallica releases: in the dust sleeve of . . . *And Justice for All*, as well as on the video box for *Cliff 'Em All.*)

Given the role of Metallica's unofficial-official artist, Pushead has also contributed artwork to such bands as Areosmith, Mötley Crüe and Prong. He also ran Pusmort, his own record label, and leads the band Septic Death.

The San Francisco–based Pushead was influenced by the comic-book styles of Berni Wrightson, who drew *Swamp Thing*; Jack Kirby, who created *The Fantastic Four*; Will Eisner who drew *The Spirit*; and Marvel Comics main-stay Alex Nino. He has also drawn for such bands as the Misfits, Blitzspeer, SS Decontrol, Corrosion of Conformity, the Necros and the Meatmen. Pushead's first album cover was Wasted Youth's *Reagan's In* album.

Pushead's art is stark and chilling, capturing the essence of the music it accompanies. His grim, weathered-skull designs for subsequent records *One* and *Harvester of Sorrow* are images hard to forget.

* * *

The Opening for Ozzy tour was accident-prone. In Evansville, Indiana, James broke his wrist in a skateboard spill. For that one concert, guitar tech James Marshall played James's parts from the side of the stage. (Marshall later went on to notoriety as a part of Seattle-based Metal Church.) Needless to say, some gigs were missed. "Me and Cliff had to go out in front of fifteen thousand people and tell them that we wouldn't be appearing that night," Lars recalled, "which was *not* the most fun thing to do. It was the first time I ever really needed a drink before I've walked out onstage anywhere."

Liquor was indeed the drug of choice during that tour, with the band's feeling that the night-after-night grind of touring requires a certain degree of partying. Lars could be seen sporting a T-shirt with the legend ALCOHOLICA/DRANK 'EM ALL, and there were even rumors that Metallica's contract had a clause that provided the band with two bottles of Absolut vodka per night.

Because of Ozzy's well-known difficulties with alcohol at that time, he tried to keep a low liquor profile. The average Metallica member's liquor intake may have caused some friction between the Ozzy and Metallica crews.

Ozzy was said to have had a mean temper when loaded, and one night Lars got a hint of it. Drinking with Ozzy, Lars asked if for some reason Ozzy washed his hair after the show. Somehow, Ozzy was insulted by this. Briefly, Lars thought the bizarre incident might have them kicked off the tour.

Ozzy may have called it The Ultimate Tour, but the name Metallica gave their half was Damage Inc. The name rang oddly true at New Jersey's Meadowlands Arena, when audience members smashed seats during Ozzy's encore. Estimated costs for the damage were set at $125,000.

On a tour with hundreds of shows, actual incidences of violence are rare, but just one Meadowlands occurrence is enough to start the drumbeats of the anti-rock forces. In 1986, the debate was still red-hot over whether rock was obscene or harmful to children. It was only the previous fall that hearings on Capitol Hill drew testimony from John Denver, from Frank Zappa and from Dee Snider of Twisted Sister. The clearinghouse for anti-rock information founded by government bureaucrats' wives, the aforementioned Parents Music Resource Center, seemed like an unthreatening little group made up of parents concerned that their kids are listening to dirty rock or rap albums. Setting aside the slippery judgmental slope of deciding what is "obscene," the PMRC protested that they never called for anything to be banned.

That may have been true, but the fact was unavoidable that every self-styled moral crusader and collection-plate charlatan in the country rallied around the PMRC. With the authority of the Washington Wives for inspiration, a new breed of ill-informed, sometimes racist, anti-rock crusaders continued to decry rock'n'roll—and heavy metal especially—as a blight on the lives of America's youth.

The PMRC kept a list of songs whose lyrics they found unacceptable, called their "Rock File." At one time, this list included Judas Priest's "Eat Me Alive," Mötley Crüe's "Bastard" and "Ten Seconds to Love," Venom's "Possessed," Black Sabbath's "Trashed," Van Halen's "Hot for Teacher," Twisted Sister's "We're Not Gonna Take It," and AC/DC's "Let Me Put My Love into You." The list also included songs by the likes of Sheena Easton and Cyndi Lauper.

A Californian Christian Fundamentalist, the Reverend Gary Greenwald, took his anti-rock message on the road, preaching to crowds that numbered in the hundreds. His sermons were often accompanied by record-smashing rites. Greenwald may have stretched the credibility of the anti-rock crusaders farther than anyone before or since, with his firm belief that Led Zeppelin's most popular hit "Stairway to Heaven" contained a backwards-masked message. The clandestine command was said to say "There's no denying it, here's to my sweet Satan." The questionable syntax involved may lead some to believe that Greenwald and his supporters were just hearing things as they carefully listened to their backwards-spun Led Zep album—much in the same way people staring at clouds think they see recognizable shapes.

There has also been no scientific verification of the Fundamentalists' claims that the human brain can actually hear a backwards message—buried in an album's mix—and miraculously play it forward to get its meaning. The most self-defeating aspect of this outrageous charge is that as an example of backwards masking bearing blasphemous instructions, the Fundamentalists chose perhaps the single most listened-to song of the last twenty years. If their hypothesis were correct, every boy and girl in America would have been sacrificing goats on an inverted pentagram instead of ordering fries-and-a-shake at Burger King.

The 1986 Ozzy tour had become a sort of battleground in the holy war waged by the anti-rock faithful. Rumors were circulating—based on stories that may well have been apocryphal—that the "satanic" rocker Ozzy Osbourne routinely bit the heads off of live bats in concert. The issue formed a peculiar anti-Ozzy alliance: right-wing Fundamentalists and left-wing animal-rights activists.

Religious groups would hand out flyers in front of Ozzy's venues, and the comparatively unknown Metallica was not targeted (although it was certainly guilty by association). In 1986, Ozzy Osbourne became known to the American population as that guy that bites the heads off of bats. Comedians used Ozzy as shorthand for all the allegedly bizarre excesses of heavy metal and youth culture in general. During the punk years, the Sex Pistols' Johnny Rotten was given a similar honor.

"With this whole censorship bullshit, like I've said before, I'm of the thought that if you ban something, it's gonna make kids want it more," Lars told journalist Harold DeMuir. "If you're 14 and you can't see an R-rated movie, that becomes an obsession. You always want what you're not allowed to have, so I see the whole censorship thing as being rather useless. It's just stupid that these people have to take fun away from other people. We leave *them* alone, why can't they leave *us* alone?"

10

> Louder and louder, wilder and wilder, mounted the shrieking and whining of that desperate viol. The player was dripping with an uncanny perspiration and twisted like a monkey, always looking frantically at the curtained window. In his frenzied strains I could almost see shadowy satyrs and bacchanals dancing and whirling insanely through seething abysses of clouds and smoke and lightning.
>
> —H. P. Lovecraft, *The Music of Erich Zann*

When the Ozzy tour closed up shop in mid-1986, Metallica continued on, this time as headliners. With their Yonkers Music Building buddies Anthrax opening up, the tour would wend its way through the British Isles, then on through Europe and ultimately to Japan. There were also festival dates, such as July's Roskilde in Denmark, which put Metallica on a bill with Eric Clapton, Elvis Costello and Big Country.

Europe had always received Metallica warmly—its audiences were more receptive to bands that didn't get on the radio. "We're getting a good draw, it's a fucking hell of a lot of fun," Cliff Burton told *Sounds,* then added, "It is painful at first, our necks and lower backs really hurt. But aspirin is a *great* drug." The touring was indeed hard, but rewarding: the Anthrax-incited audiences would roar in unison along with "Seek and Destroy," and become a shimmering sea of lighters for "Welcome Home (Sanitarium)." The Metallica tour rolled on and the Jägermeister flowed like, well, Jägermeister.

On September 27, 1986, on the Scandinavian leg of the tour, the band had finished up their Stockholm show. In the predawn hours, the Metallica bus was already roaring towards the ferry for Copenhagen for their next date.

On a stretch of highway in Ljungby, Sweden, the bus suddenly swerved off the road. As it hit the highway skirting, it tipped over, toppling into a ditch. Cliff Burton, asleep in one of the bunks, was thrown through the window by the jolt of the tipping bus. In a split second, the bus rolled over Cliff, killing him instantly.

The first confused, horrified minutes after the crash were marked by disbelief, followed by shock. The shock was more than the psychological kind for some: Lars had broken some bones in his foot and tour manager Bobby Schneider dislocated his shoulder. Some were unable to crawl out of the bus for a time, while many of those who did stood stunned in the chill Swedish night wearing only their underwear.

According to the driver, he'd hit a patch of ice that came up on him too fast to be avoided. James remembered running up and down the side of the road in his shock and grief, desperately *looking* for the patch of ice the driver had blamed. He never found the ice, but later wondered if he'd really wanted to find it in the first place.

James had very nearly met the same fate as Cliff that night. "I couldn't sleep in those bunks. I usually slept in the one next to Cliff," James told *Creem Metal*. "But that night I couldn't because it was too drafty. It was screwing up my

Cliff Burton. Courtesy Krasner/Trebitz.

voice and I was getting sick." It may well have been an illness that saved his life.

Hours later, the weary, shell-shocked band and crew were finished being treated at a Swedish hospital. As usual, it was the tour manager's job to round the band up to move out. James recalled to *Rolling Stone* that the tour manager said, " 'We're going to get a cab for the band.' And when he said 'the band,' it was like 'Oh, God, the band? We're not a band right now.' "

In the days following Cliff's death, the band returned to San Francisco, got back together with their girlfriends and tried to sort things out. Spending time with Cliff's family and friends did a lot to help Lars, James and Kirk with their grief.

Jon and Marsha Zazula were some of the first to hear of Cliff's death, because of Anthrax's proximity to the accident. (Coincidentally, they were in San Francisco to see Testament, whom they would later sign.) Like everyone, they were shocked by the abrupt, chilling end to a young, dear friend. But the Zazulas remembered a Cliff Burton who was not some metal wild man of rock legend, but rather a kind, intelligent individual. When the rest of the band was overzealously whooping it up, it was Cliff who'd sit the Zazulas' little daughter on his lap and read her stories. Jon and Marsha would miss him deeply.

As Michael Alago remembers Cliff, "He always had this strong, dark presence to him where you *did* just look up to him because he was an incredible player and a very funny, wonderful human being."

In her excellent study of suburban heavy metal kids, *Teenage Wasteland,* Donna Gaines writes of a die-hard Metallica fan named Jackie who had several tattoos with band-related themes. One tattoo, a tribute to Cliff, depicted a headstone with an electric bass hanging on it. Dave Mustaine also remembered Cliff in his own way, with the song "In My Darkest Hour," featured on Megadeth's *So Far . . . So Good . . . So What!* album.

When James Hetfield was asked if the death of Cliff Burton would steer him away from death-related themes in future Metallica songs, he told *Rolling Stone,* "Man, those lyrics mean a lot more to me now."

On the night before Cliff Burton's funeral, the remaining Metallica members held a meeting, along with managers Peter Mensch and Cliff Burnstein. As Lars recalled to *Musician,* "We have had very few meetings, but the night before Cliff's funeral we sat down and said, 'Okay, what are we gonna do now?' "

Despite their desolation over Cliff's terrible, premature death, there was very little thought of letting the group disintegrate. Rather, they tried to assess what needed to be done. "We had our first Japanese tour booked for November, and we thought that if we left those dates in, it would put pressure on us to get it back together," Lars remembered to Harold DeMuir. "I know Cliff, more than anyone else in the band, would have been the first guy to give us a kick in the ass, and wouldn't want us to sit around. It's what *he* would have wanted us to do.

"The spirit of this band has always been about fighting on, against all the shit that we've always run into," Lars continued to DeMuir. "Obviously, there's never been anything like *this* before, but now we can have even more incentive to carry on and do what we have to do. . . . The only time we've looked back on the accident is when we've talked about it in interviews."

Feelings of loss for Cliff were made more complex with the vague sense of betrayal felt when looking for a lost friend's replacement. Of course, "replacement" is the

wrong word for it. Indeed, Cliff's personality was so perva-
sive and so much a part of the group consciousness that
there was never a thought given to finding, as Lars put it,
"Cliff Burton II." They wanted a bassist who could blend
into the already-established Metallica sound.

"I'm a little surprised at how fast we did it, but we've
always been about following instinct," Lars told DeMuir.
"Basically, what happened is that, after the accident, we
had over four months of touring left to do. And we decided
that it would be good for us to leave the Japanese dates
in, as a way of putting pressure on ourselves to get our
shit together. The Japanese dates started on November 15,
which gave us three weeks from the time we met up again
for the funeral."

When the band first considered players for audition,
they had a notion to hire some hotshot, young-gun bassist.
They had no interest in a journeyman player with a mile-
long résumé.

"We initially thought that we would maybe just get a
temporary replacement for the tour, and then get a permanent replacement after that," Lars continued to DeMuir. "But
[at our] meeting in San Francisco the night before the funeral,
[we] decided to use the three weeks to find a permanent
replacement. We had a week's worth of auditions, and we
could've auditioned 8,000 more people, but we followed
our instincts and made our decision."

When considering a bass player, the band had other
than just musical considerations. They also felt it important
that the new member be honest and be able to fit in socially
with the others. Bands are usually much more like families
than just some aggregation of coworkers.

The period spent auditioning new bass players, in
Lars's opinion, helped the band through their mourning for

Cliff. It has even been said by band members that they probably *would've* broken up if they hadn't busied themselves with this specific project.

The list of auditioning bass players includes a number who'd go on to fame in other bands. They included bassmen from such outfits as Vio-lence, Testament, Culprit, Laaz Rockit, Heathen, Prong, Abattoir, Blind Illusion and even Kirk's friend Les Claypool from Primus. (Metallica asked Joey Vera of Armored Saint to audition, but he declined.)

After the cast-of-thousands, dog-and-pony-show auditions were over, the list had been narrowed to just two. Each of the players were asked to spend a day rehearsing with Metallica. But Lars Ulrich had been pretty sure all along that Jason Newsted from Flotsam and Jetsam was their new bass player. "We played a few numbers with Jason," Lars remembered, "and then we all sort of went to the bathroom and in low voices stood there, whispering to each other, *'That's the guy.'*"

Jason Newsted was born on March 4, 1963, in Battle Creek, Michigan. Jason's father was a foreign documents manager for an equipment company, and his mother—amusingly enough—worked for a hearing aid center.

When Jason turned fourteen, he persuaded his father to buy him an electric bass, the instrument of Gene Simmons, his favorite Kiss member. After playing the bass for a while, he put it away, and became far more involved with riding and tending to the family's horses. When the Newsteds moved from Battle Creek to Phoenix, Arizona, in 1981, the horses did not come with them. And Jason rediscovered his electric bass.

Never professing any secret desire—as some bassists

do—to be a guitar player, Jason's four-string heroes were Geezer Butler of Black Sabbath, Chris Squire of Yes, Lemmy Kilmister of Motörhead and especially Geddy Lee of Rush.

In Phoenix, Jason and three friends founded a metal band called Flotsam and Jetsam. Before long, Flotsam and Jetsam would come before the notice of Brian Slagel of Metal Blade Records. When Metal Blade artists toured the Southwest, Flotsam and Jetsam was a frequent local-band opening act. "They opened for everybody," recalls Brian Slagel. "A couple of bands came back and said, 'Gosh, you should really check out this band Flotsam and Jetsam from Phoenix. They're really good.''

When Brian Slagel got interested in the band, he started dealing with the group's unofficial manager and spokesperson, Jason Newsted. "He did everything, was the band leader, basically," Slagel remembers, and added, "All the guys in the band were great guys. Easy to deal with, a lot of fun, no problems. Jason had it together, too. He knew what he was doing and he was really good at promoting the band. They did a lot of promotion around Phoenix and they also sent out demo tapes to magazines and things. He was really good at that."

Brian Slagel trekked out to Phoenix to see Flotsam and Jetsam firsthand. A few of the band members were living in a big rented house in Phoenix, with an especially comfortable rehearsal space in the garage.

After seeing Flotsam and Jetsam, Slagel didn't take much convincing. "We got a demo tape and we put 'em on one of our *Metal Massacre* compilations and it did really well," he remembered. "Went out and saw them and they were great. We said, 'Hey, let's do a record.' "

The record that Flotsam and Jetsam recorded for Metal Blade was called *Doomsday for the Deceiver*. Produced by

Brian Slagel, *Doomsday* is an energized, all-out thrash assault, still worthy of a listen today, especially such tracks as "Metalshock," "U.S.L.W.," the instrumental "Flotzilla," and especially "Iron Tears," a nasty thrasher with a majestic chorus.

The title track seems most influenced by Metallica—it's an elaborate, multipart composition with lyrical, buzzing acoustic guitars. And strangely enough, the album also includes a song called "Fade to Black." The liner notes thank those bands most influential to them: Motörhead, KISS, AC/DC . . . and Metallica.

In a strange way, Flotsam and Jetsam followed Metallica's label trail. Making their debut on a Metal Blade *Massacre* compilation, the band was later signed to Elektra Records by A&R man Michael Alago. Alago, who had also signed Metal Church, Public Image Ltd. and Alan Vega to Elektra, had been interested in them throughout 1986. Alago had extensive dealings with Jason, and had flown out to Phoenix to see the band on their home turf. The band was in the process of signing with Elektra when Cliff was killed.

As the unofficial accountant for Flotsam and Jetsam, Jason's departure was a double headache for the band. When Jason was ready to leave to join Metallica, he showed his mates what the finance books looked like and was soon gone. He admits that the Flotsam crew thought less than kindly of him after that, but their fences were said to be mended later on.

When Jason joined Metallica, he'd been living in his band's rehearsal shed on a subsistence diet that centered around peanut butter sandwiches. In Metallica, the money was sure to be better, but the challenges were unimaginable.

Jason's first conversations with Lars led Jason to believe that he had a very good shot at making the cut. Jason learned Cliff's bass parts note-for-note, which wasn't that hard, since Flotsam and Jetsam used to play certain Metallica songs as covers. During the actual audition, Jason played the Cliff parts, but made sure to stick in a few signs that he had some ideas of his own. (When Jason plays the older songs, he tries to stick closely to Cliff's original parts.)

Jason believed that his abilities as a songwriter gave him an edge over the other hopefuls. By Jason's own estimate, he wrote about half the music and most of the words for Flotsam and Jetsam. As Jason told *Hit Parader,* there had been "forty to sixty guys from all over the country who wanted to be in this group, but there were a couple of things Metallica wanted, and writing was definitely one of them."

"Metallica is the ultimate. . . . There was no way I'd ever turn down the chance to play with Metallica, because it's a dream come true for me," Jason told Harold DeMuir. "Flotsam was influenced heavily by Metallica. Flotsam also has a lot of weird timing; and the stamina, the speed and the chords were similar."

Jason hoped to start writing songs for Metallica. His respect for his bandmates' abilities is well documented. As Jason told *Hit Parader,* "James Hetfield is really a genius. He can come up with the heaviest chunking riffs, then turn around and do something classical and pretty that makes you tingle. This band is really the upper sector of musicians."

"The best part about Metallica is that there really aren't any big egos at work here," Jason told the same publication. "Everyone's just interested in making good music."

In October of 1986, about one month after the accident that claimed Cliff Burton's life, Jason Newsted was hired as Metallica's new bassist. "I feel that Jason's presence has given us a whole new breath of fresh air," Lars remarked to Harold DeMuir. "His excitement and his natural yahoo-ness about the whole thing has given the three of us a good kick in the ass, and sort of spilled over on us, and we're even more willing than before. Obviously, everything that happened is tragic, but we have to look ahead and not keep looking back. I think Jason's excitement about the whole thing has given us a sort of second wind. Everything is cool."

With new bassist Jason Newsted, Metallica embarked on a ten-day tour of Japan in November of 1986. The Japanese fans were ecstatic. They presented the band with cartoon caricatures of themselves, drawn in classic Japanese-cartoon style. (Comic-collecting Japanophile Kirk must've gotten some kick out of that.) Jason recalls that during these first dates with the band, he'd see the unfurling of banners proclaiming "CIIFF R.I.P.—WELCOME JASON." They were a warm reassurance he wouldn't soon forget.

Another thing that Jason would never forget was the nearly continual hazing he faced from the rest of the band. Loads of sushi and gallons of saki were charged to Jason's room. The band would pile in one cab for sight-seeing and force Jason to travel on his own. The rest of the band teased Jason by calling him Carole—after Carole King, to whom he does bear a "fleeting" resemblance. (Best not to dwell upon on whom that reflects worse.)

When the tour took the band to New York, a friend of Kirk's had sent him a case of liquor, which the band members proceeded to drink. Then, with much booze behind them, they got the idea to visit Jason in the middle of the night. They knocked repeatedly on his door, but Jason, sleeping with earplugs in, was oblivious. Inventively, the band told the building's doorman that Jason was inside, and—in classic rock star fashion—was choking on his own vomit and needed immediate assistance. They kicked Jason's door in, trashed the room and sprayed him with shaving cream. Jason, determined not to be rattled, said nothing.

"They taunted and teased him and harassed him and made him feel not a part of the band at all," Michael Alago remembers. "But they're crazy like that, they're children. He couldn't write with them, he came in to play his parts when *they* told him he was coming in to play his parts. And Jason turned into a very very strong individual. He just stood up to all the pressure that the boys in the band heaped upon him and now he really is one of the guys. He's grown tremendously as a bass player and he looks amazing and he's one of the guys now."

Lars's explained this treatment as ensuring that Jason wouldn't get a swelled head over joining such a hip band. (It is more likely that Jason was wondering if Flotsam and Jetsam would take him back.) The Metallica philosophy, as stated by Lars, tries to keep arrogant rock star behavior to a bare minimum. As Lars also commented to *Creem Metal* about Jason, "He's a little gullible at times, which makes it kind of fun."

The hazing, by Jason's estimate, lasted a full year, yet he was determined not to let it get him down. Years later, Lars recognized that the endless tormenting of Jason Newsted was a reflection of their *own* inability to cope with the loss of Cliff Burton.

Despite the fan acceptance that was so welcome, Jason still felt the burden of history when he took a bass solo. As he told *Guitar Player*, "I get really nervous when the solo shit comes around. Cliff's solos were absolutely brilliant, so I always feel a bit weird." When not soloing, Jason tried to stick to his basic bass lines—not to cram bass fills into any available space, as Cliff tended to. (Jason also played with a pick, as opposed to Cliff, who played with his fingers. Some feel that a pick gives the bass a tighter sound.)

On the day after Thanksgiving 1986, a saki-sodden Metallica began a headlining tour of the United States. For the fans who got interested in the band during the Ozzy tour, Metallica came back stronger than ever with a setlist that included "Whiplash," "The Thing That Should Not Be," "Battery," and "Fight Fire with Fire."

When the band played Detroit, the show nearest Jason's first hometown of Battle Creek, many of Jason's friends and family had turned out for the show. In general, things went pretty well, although Jason couldn't have been pleased that James threw up several times during the concert.

In the first weeks of 1987, Metallica completed the month of European concerts that went unplayed in the wake of Cliff Burton's death. At one Essen, West Germany, concert in late January, the band was joined by members of Metal Church, including Metallica's former guitar roadie James Marshall. The Metal Churchmen came out for the last few songs, and banged out a few Metal Church tunes while they were at it.

The last date of the Master of Puppets tour was finally played on February 13, 1987, in the Swedish town of Gothenburg. Lars said that the band had been "on the road for almost a year. After that, we decided to take a couple of weeks away from music."

When the tour was over, the band members split off in different directions. Lars headed for London, James went back to his East Bay home for some traditional R&R, and Kirk went shopping for toys. When Jason returned to Phoenix, he could be reasonably sure that the worst of his trials were over, and that at least Metallica's audience was happy with him. "The acceptance of the fans is just incredible," Jason told *Faces.* "No one can ever be Cliff Burton, especially not me. But they like Jason Newsted all the same. It gets more and more comfortable all the time."

11

> "Citizens of Gravity we are converting all out to Heavy Metal. Carbonic Plague of the Vegetable People threatens our Heavy Metal State. Report to your nearest Plating Station. It's fun to be plated."
>
> —William Burroughs,
> *The Soft Machine*

The life of a rock band is far more predictable than most people think. They make albums. They tour to support those albums. When the tour is over, they'd better start thinking about the next album, 'cause nobody's paying 'em to sit around and drink.

This was more or less the case with Metallica when they returned to the Bay Area after completing the Master of Puppets tour.

By March of 1987, with very little time for posttour decompression, Metallica rented time at a well-appointed rehearsal studio in affluent Marin County. Lars recalled of the facility: "Next door to us we had Night Ranger, then on the other side of us we had Starship—you know, one of *those* kind of places."

On the first day of rehearsal, the band goofed around—who could expect more on a first day back— playing every NWOBHM tune they could scrape together. This kind of party-band attitude was supposed to help them loosen up for the serious songwriting that was before them.

On the second day of rehearsal, they tried playing each other's instruments. Playing lots of cover tunes was one thing, but no one could really explain what benefit would come from playing each other's instruments. It seemed like fun. It also seemed like they were feeling the tiniest bit uncomfortable in such a flashy rehearsal space, where they were *literally* surrounded by tired corporate rock acts.

Despite their failure to do any meaningful work so far, and beating God by four days, Metallica rested on the third day.

On the fourth day, James Hetfield went skateboarding in Oakland in a primo spot for 'boarders—an empty swimming pool. James must have been enjoying himself profoundly, but whether it was a failure to get vertical or actual success, an excess of zeal once again left James with an arm broken—in not one but two places this time. Metal plates were put into his arm to immobilize it during its healing period.

James's arm would take two and a half months to mend, and during this time, his contributions to the band were limited, to say the least.

But this was a mere temporary setback. The Metallicans knew that if they were ever going to get anything written, they'd have to leave that well-upholstered coffin and get back to their roots. Like most workaday rock bands, Metallica was used to a more *traditional* rehearsal facility—a garage.

With James out of commission, the band took the opportunity of his accident to repair to the two-car garage behind

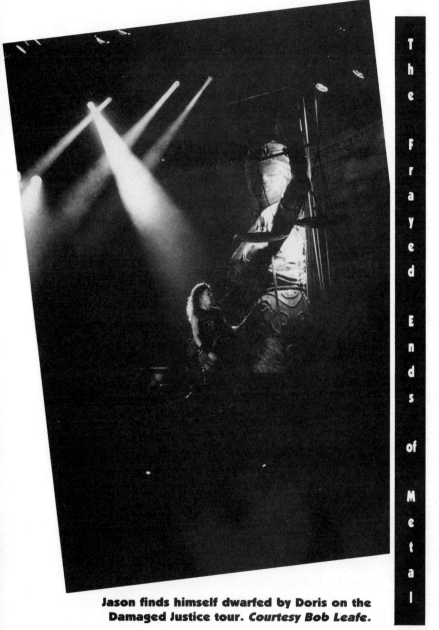

Jason finds himself dwarfed by Doris on the Damaged Justice tour. *Courtesy Bob Leafe.*

Lars's East Bay home. There they would carve out a new rehearsal space, and then get to work on the new songs.

Over a six-week period in April and May of 1987, the band worked the garage like they were hosting some heavy metal version of *This Old House*. They wanted the new rehearsal space to be the same kind of relaxed, low-pressure refuge as the one in the house Lars and James had lived in together—but this time with soundproofing superior to the egg cartons and carpeting that lined the old place.

Jason, whose Phoenix rehearsal garage had been such a showcase, took the lead in Lars's garage conversion. Jason was often there before Lars got up. "I came down to help out every day when I woke up, about two P.M.," Lars explained. "James would come over and do whatever he could with his arm being broken, and Kirk was out doing his toy shopping!"

For Metallica, a garage is more than just a place to park your car. It could also be that the garage, an enclosed area, is there to shield them from the demands of the outside world—or the music business.

As a creative place, the rock musician's garage is nearly symbolic. It's akin to the woodshed of the serious jazz musician. Either one is a place where the musician goes to shut out the noise—and make some of his own.

"We came off the road from the Puppets tour in February '87 and made a couple of measly attempts to get back in the mode of songwriting over the course of, like, spring and summer," Lars notes. "With our band, the way it works, we can't really force the writing. It's not like you go check in somewhere and say, 'We'll write Monday through Friday between three and seven P.M.' It doesn't work like that."

One of the many good things about garages is that you never have to book time in one. "We started jamming in the garage—we hadn't played together for so long, and in true

Metallica fashion we started playing all these stupid cover versions," Lars remembered. "And the more we played some of these cover songs, the more fun it was to play them. It seemed like a cool thing to do, to initiate the garage by doing all these covers, to get back into the habit of playing together."

But by July of that year, these nostalgic, rocking reveries were starting to be taken a bit more seriously. As Lars commented, "We thought it would be quite cool to record this stuff—obviously as just a fun thing to do, having these bullshit songs slaughtered by Metallica."

Back in 1981, before Brian Slagel decided to compile the first *Metal Massacre* album, all Lars and James wanted to do was to sit around and play their favorite metal covers. By the time 1987 had rolled around, that's *still* all these guys wanted to do.

The idea was this: to record these cover tunes in the studio with the same raw, loose attitude that made the garage so much fun. In early July, the band left for L.A.'s A & M recording studios. With no producer on the date (the album sleeve said NOT VERY PRODUCED BY METALLICA), the only techie on the project was engineer Csaba Petocz, who kept an eye on the sound levels.

The *Garage Days Rerevisited* EP begins with "Helpless," a Diamond Head tune from 1980. It's a booming vocal performance from James, singing against the song's lurching, climbing chords.

Next is Holocaust song "Small Hours," whose lumbering, leaden-footed stomp turns into a galloping NWOBHM charger, and then redescends back into the sonic sludge.

Perhaps the oddest cover in the set is "The Wait," originally released in 1980 by London-based Killing Joke. Turning up in the late seventies, Killing Joke created a decidedly dark-hued but invigorating blend of metal, punk and art-rock. Often distorting his vocals, lead singer Jaz Coleman usually took listeners on a highly danceable journey to the end of the world. "The Wait" was from Killing Joke's self-titled debut album, generally thought to be their best.

Metallica's treatment of "The Wait" is quite faithful, echoing the original's tense, ravenous and irresistible guitar lick. James's processed vocals sail into the clarion-call chorus as mounting guitars add to the general air of claustrophobia.

"Crash Course in Brain Surgery," for which Metallica court artist Pushead designed a T-shirt, was originally recorded by Budgie in the early seventies. A pummelingly powerful Welsh band, Budgie is one of the unheralded pioneers of savage seventies metal. Still recording into the eighties, Budgie was among the heaviest metal of its day.

"Crash Course in Brain Surgery," centered around an oddly shaped, unspooling riff, is another heavy, clunking rocker that the band surely wishes it had written.

The EP ends with a medley of "The Last Caress" and "Green Hell," both by New Jersey fright-punkers the Misfits. Led by the charismatic Glenn Danzig, the Misfits had a knack for horror-movie gore and anthemic punktunes. Among the great, instant sing-along gems on their seminal 1982 *Walk Among Us* album are "Astro-Zombies," "When I Turned into a Martian" and a sensitive memoir entitled "Mommy, Can I Go Out and Kill Tonight?"

In 1984, when the Misfits broke up, Danzig and bassist Eerie Von formed Samhain, a darker, dirgier, more biblical and less cartoonish concept. With Samhain's demise a couple of years later, Danzig made his life simpler and named his new band Danzig. Now recording for Rick Rubin's Def American Records—home of Slayer—Danzig continues to explore his own stark, metallic vision of the evil side of rock.

Danzig's dark sense of humor was apparent on his Long Way Back from Hell tour, where he made his laminated backstage passes in the shape of inverted crosses. Since everyone has to wear them, these laminates made the back-stage crowds look like a satanists' convention.

James and Cliff's Misfits-mania—after all, Cliff sported a Misfits tattoo on his right shoulder—has resulted in a Misfits-Samhain-Danzig subcult amongst Metallica fans. Because of Samhain's short life span, those items and other artifacts are worn by Metallica fans like badges of honor. Glenn Danzig, like Kirk Hammett, is a rabid comic book and toy collector. When they're in the same town, Glenn and Kirk have been known to go out together in search of pop cultural oddities.

"Last Caress" is a classic Misfits punk-pop anthem, and "Green Hell" is driven by a faster, more hardcore rhythm. You do get the impression that Metallica did two Misfits songs together because they just couldn't bring themselves to record something short.

What would finally be called the The $5.98 EP: Garage Days Rerevisited went from conception to completion in no more than a month—an incredibly quick project by any band's standards. The price was included in the title to remind retailers that this was only an EP—not an LP—and should be priced accordingly.

Liner notes told the story of the Garage Days Rerevisited sessions in what looks like Lars's handwriting—or at least the words certainly sound like his. The EP also features a Ross Halfin photo of each band member. In mock publicity-shot style, the Metallicans wrote their autographs—with names deliberately misspelled—on each photo.

Like a case of opening-night jitters, Lars did have a sneaking fear that the informal nature of the covers-only set would be lost on some fans. He was afraid they'd hear the EP's unpolished, near-demo-quality and conclude that the band had started turning out low-quality product.

Lars had little to worry about, however. The *Garage Days Rerevisited* EP was released in August of 1987. By December of that year, the EP had gone gold.

Another reason for the existence of *Garage Days Rerevisited* EP was given on an MTV call-in show with Lars and Kirk. "We were playing a Castle Donington gig in London and also two other gigs in Germany and we wanted to put out something," said Kirk, "some sort of product so that it would tie in with these shows. And when Elektra found out about it, they decided—you know—'Let's get a part of that.' And they released it in the States and that's how that all came about."

And so it was with a new release in hand that Metallica returned to Castle Donington for a Monsters of Rock show on August 18, 1987. Also featured on the date was Bon Jovi, Dio, Anthrax, W.A.S.P. and Cinderella. Which just goes to show that from little garages, great things often grow. And they aren't always that huge circular grease spot.

12

The 1987–88 period marked one of the band's longest breaks from the road. It was as though the Metalliguys had better check first to see if they still had personal lives waiting for them before they got back to the Bay Area.

After months and months of making their own music, Metallica found great solace in other people doing the music making for a change. Lars has been quoted that Metallica's taste in music would probably surprise their listeners, with such unlikely choices as R.E.M., Kate Bush, Peter Gabriel, Sisters of Mercy, U2 and Roxy Music. On a more reassuringly metallic note, their rugged sound systems have been known to blast the likes of Thin Lizzy, early Sabbath, Iron Maiden, Rush, ZZ Top, Queen, and the Cult. On a punkier tip, neighbors could be calling the police over GBH, Killing Joke, Discharge, Black Flag or Samhain. Still, for a night of drunken revelry, Lars has suggested that nothing beats the Misfits.

By the late eighties, the boundaries of metal, punk and other alternative styles were being blurred—something for which Metallica could claim some responsibility. "We pushed underground metal out," Kirk told *Sounds*. "The people who were into it needed something to focus on, and we provided that. I think the scene's dying now, people used to collect and swap tapes of gigs, but it's saturated, the whole genre is sub-divided into little titles now, like street-metal."

But guitarists go on forever, and Kirk would still listen to not only Jeff Beck and Michael Schenker, but also the semimystical Uli Jon Roth, from whom he believes Youngest Guitar God Yngwie Malmsteen learned a great deal.

Less conventionally, though, Kirk has professed great respect for radical rap groups Public Enemy and N.W.A. Where the violent images of "gangsta rap" have intimidated many, Kirk believes that the "ugliness" or "hardness" of the rap message is just neutral observation. The angry scenarios explored in many metal songs have met similar reactions to those of hardcore rap.

James Hetfield's taste in rap is limited to white L.A. rap-rockers the Red Hot Chili Peppers, as well as hard-rock stalwarts Aerosmith. Punk-leaning James also acquired a taste for the New York thrash-punks the Cro-Mags. The Cro-Mags, like Texans-in-San-Francisco D.R.I., were punks who sank deeper and deeper into metal with every new release. The leader of the Cro-Mags was a Hare Krishna and some have likened their guitar sound to Purple-era Ritchie Blackmore.

At almost the opposite extreme, Jason Newsted often prefers black music on the order of reggae and the classic soul of such Motown artists as Marvin Gaye, the Four Tops and the Temptations. Not averse to sudden shifts towards Tom Waits or even Mozart, Jason still returns to Sabbath or Zeppelin.

Lars Ulrich, ever the metal traditionalist, also finds present-day metal a bit hard to bear. "Apart from a few exceptions, most of the stuff that's been coming out lately is really tired old repetitions of itself," he told *Circus*. "A lot of music from the '70s still stands up today and sounds as majestic and as fresh and as great as it did back then." Not a complete curmudgeon, Lars has praised highly Slayer's *Reign in Blood* as an album to get lost in, especially with headphones on. Lars has indicated that headphones are one of the most important inventions ever.

During this time, James administered an informal joke band with the typically tasteless name of Spastic Children. The Stone club was most often the venue, with James and Kirk handling guitar duties. One song they did was entitled "Bra Section" and recalls the lustful gaze of a little kid ogling the lingerie models in clothing catalogs. Another was entitled "Brief Star Wars Army." They were proud to tell anyone who'd listen that Spastic Children never practice.

At one Spastic Children set at the Stone, James and Kirk tried to play their encore completely naked. The club told them they'd be permanently banned if they did it, so the encore was played, somewhat anticlimactically, in their underwear.

Another *béorscipe* music crew gathered from time to time at a nearby ranch, informally called the Maxwell House Ranch. Organized by James, Faith No More guitarist Jim Martin and his brother Lou Martin, friends would casually barbecue or jam, when not just sitting out on the porch. Their preferred potation was port—or porch, which they felt was a more practical name for it.

The Maxwell House Ranch band made up songs on fairly disgusting topics, including one song about released convict Larry Singleton, who had been imprisoned for raping a young California girl and chopping her arms off. (A number of local communities were in the news for trying to keep Singleton from moving there after his eventual release from prison.) The Larry Singleton song was akin to the *National Lampoon* humor of horrifying bad taste in the seventies.

Metallica's close bond with their fans could have something to do with the band's refusal to endorse the time-honored rock star–rock fan clichés. "We're no different from them. We see the world like other people," Lars remarked to *Metallix*. "We don't live in huge mansions, and we're not hiding behind fences and making our own pretentious fantasy world with chicks and mountains of drugs. We live in the real world."

James Hetfield doesn't need a fence. "I just walk out with the gun and say, 'Hey!,'" he told *Circus*. "Oh, yeah, I'm a meanie. I send my dogs after 'em. . . . No, actually, I just tell 'em, 'This is my house and . . . leave me alone, okay?'" The kids in James's town know where he lives, but, with the exception of the occasional trespasser, are usually pretty low-key about it.

Clubbing stopped being as much fun as it used to be once James started being more widely recognized. "Sometimes going out to rock clubs isn't a very good idea," he told *Circus*. "You can't really sit down and have a quiet beer, shoot some pool. . . ."

James—and some of his bandmates—have a far better time in Bay Area strip clubs, where they are usually left alone, although welcoming the disturbance of on-the-house beers.

Sticking close to street-level, James has expressed his occasional uneasiness with the large amounts of money that come from being in a best-selling rock band. This may be why he keeps his Recording Industry Association of America–certified gold records on the wall of his storage shed. James also often feels out of place in fancy hotels.

Preferring solitude or the company of close friends, his favorite pastime is wilderness duck-hunting trips. Although professing no racial prejudice, James's love of guns and hunting and his family roots in Nebraska may be behind his willingness to kiddingly refer to himself as a redneck.

Kirk's multicultural impulses have left him enamored of Japanica—especially Japanese comics and toys. Other American artifacts that Kirk likes to collect include plastic glue-'em-together modeling kits. Two proud purchases included a model kit of the monster from the 1958 science fiction film *It! The Terror from Beyond Space* and a Frankenstein paint-by-numbers kit.

Cliff Burton left Kirk with an admiration for H. P. Lovecraft, but Kirk also enjoys Victorian-influenced illustrator Edward Gorey, *Conan*-creator Robert E. Howard and horrormasters Clive Barker, Ramsey Campbell and Stephen King.

In December of 1987, Kirk married Rebecca, his girlfriend since 1982. (Kirk has acknowledged that Metallica was sometimes a burden to the relationship.) Kirk and Rebecca lived in a Bay Area rental home complete with a swimming pool and thirty rosebushes.

Jason was also engaged, and would later marry Judy, in December of the following year in her hometown of Minier, Illinois.

Basketball provides a physical release for Jason's more athletic pursuits, as does mountain-bike riding. A notorious caffeine-head, Jason loves his cappuccino, and has even been known to drink the supercaffeinated soft drink Jolt.

Jason has a gun collection consisting of handguns and rifles. He prefers the less restrictive gun laws of Arizona to those of California, and often goes rabbit hunting at the Maxwell House Ranch with James.

Lars, like Jason and Kirk, also got married in the late

eighties—to English-born Debbie—and the two moved into a home in North Berkeley.

"Lars—he's the consumate rock star/manager," Ron Quintana recalls. "Like Jason, he was so good at promoting his band. He always kinda acted like a rock star and always kinda figured he would be. And he's lovin' it, I'm sure. It's what he always wanted to do. He's probably the happiest guy in the band."

Lars once remarked that he could use some of his downtime flexing old muscles on the celebrity tennis circuit. Needless to say, Lars's present associates don't hit the courts very often.

Still, for much of Lars's time away from music, something inside him wishes he was back doing music. As 1987 rolled to a close, he ended up doing more of it than he might have imagined.

13

> **"Today we think about him a lot and talk about him, even joke about him. I often think—now more than ever—how much of a character and a personality Cliff actually was. He was just one in five billion people on this earth, and we will never, ever, even be tempted to come up with anyone like him."**
>
> **—Lars Ulrich, on Cliff Burton (*Creem Metal*)**

Metallica's first venture into the world of rock video would be characteristic—a ninety-minute home movie with lamentable sound quality and with video footage mostly compiled from fans' bootlegs, shot illegally with smuggled cameras. Metallica's entrance into the longform music-video market, their *$19.98 Home Vid Cliff 'Em All!*, was a rough-hewn portrait of the band while Cliff Burton walked among them.

"We don't want this video to overdo the tribute thing," Lars explained to *Hit Parader*, "but we feel it would be kinda cool to put out a visual account of when Cliff was in the band." Lars was always careful, in interviews, not to give the project the barest hint of Dead Rock Star Exploitation—a distasteful vice of the music industry.

Lars began the task of assembling material in early 1987, usually calling up the fans who shot the videos himself.

(Knowing that artists are usually incensed over illegal taping, how many of them thought twice about owning up to making the video?)

Lars acquired the footage gradually, in dribs and drabs throughout the first half of the year. Over the summer, the editing process began. The video's sound couldn't be improved too much over its original through-the-tiny-little-mike quality. By the standards of other concert longforms or one-song video clips, the low fidelity of *Cliff 'Em All!* was unconscionable. But, as any fan could tell you, it's just a *bootleg*, man. Nobody ever said this was gonna sound great. If you're a fan, it won't matter to you.

The video was directed—or more accurately, the assembly of the video was directed—by respected music video veterans Jean Pellerin and Doug Freel. Its producers were Curt Marvis and Jeff Richter.

Actually, there is some professional (often unintentionally semiprofessional) footage on *Cliff 'Em All!* Songs shot at Germany's Metal Hammer Fest were at least two-camera setups with dissolve/fade capability, although the sound is occasionally pocked. For the "Seek and Destroy" segment of the tape, the German videographers ludicrously crammed in every needless video effect you could hope to see in one place. Effects were brought to a minimum for the footage of a Cliff Burton solo that has a rocking, Hendrix-like edge, yet with a kind of folkiness. (Maybe Cliff Burton's genius was in letting each of us hear what we want in his solos.)

Tape of Metallica playing "For Whom the Bell Tolls" at an August 1985 Day on the Green in the Bay Area fares far better, with some footage shot by MTV. Starting off with a wild Cliff Burton solo, this performance clip documents a true compliment to Metallica from the hometown crowd.

James rocks Moscow at the Tushino Airfield show.
Courtesy East News-Sipa.

Still, the heart of *Cliff 'Em All!* is the fans' bootleg videos, despite the occasional amateurish zooming made immortal in *Wayne's World*.

The earliest footage on the tape goes all the way back to Dave Mustaine's tenure as lead guitarist, with a March 1983 gig at San Francisco's the Stone. Only Cliff's second date with the band, yet his solo on "Anesthesia" has a neoclassical, Zappaesque flavor—followed by a wild, blues-boogie romp. Cliff's sound was a mutation of the conventional bass: it combined bass, guitar and cello all in one. After Lars kicks in at the drum kit and James and Dave jump back in, the sound recalls a late sixties acid jam in the Cream mode.

Evidence of Jon and Marsha Zazula's foiled attempt to make a music video is seen on *Cliff 'Em All*, shot in Chicago from the Kill 'Em All for One tour. Despite a bit of video glitching here and there, the tape is indispensible for fans, with Flying V–equipped James and Kirk leading Cliff and Lars through burning versions of "No Remorse" and "Metal Militia."

The best is the short tragic vignette of Kirk and The Trouble with Feedback. After creating a torrent of guitar noise, Kirk proceeded to shake his instrument over the heads of the appreciative crowd. Someone appreciated Kirk's guitar a bit too much, and yanked it out of his hands by the strap. With the guitar seemingly still blasting away, a bemused Kirk stood there, appearing to wonder if he'd ever see it again. Moments later, he was given a new Flying V while harried roadies wrestled the guitar out of the crowd.

Their "Damage, Inc." opening-for-Ozzy tour was also featured at some length on *Cliff 'Em All*. On such songs as "Creeping Death," the spidery-armed Cliff was headbanging mightily, one foot up on the monitor.

Even amateur video can have its artistic moments, such

as the sight of Cliff nearly silhouetted with his long-necked Rickenbacker. Images of Cliff, with his seventeenth-century-length hair juxtaposed with the crosslike pegs of the bass, gave him the look of a mystic, witch-finding Puritan. And from the 1986 Roskilde Festival, powerful in-concert footage of James playing in front of a solid wall of Marshalls is a classic heavy metal image.

Of the nonmusical moments of the *Cliff 'Em All* tape, some space is devoted to some public-access cable-quality interviews with James and Cliff, each wearing a different Misfits T-shirt. Scrapes on James's face speak of pavement-kissing skateboarding disasters.

In one March '83 interview, the unidentified interviewer describes Metallica as the "hot new heavy metal band from L.A." Cliff can't contain his incredulity at her insipid remark, laughing involuntarily.

The video also showed a good number of still photos of Cliff to help capture his irreverent, open-hearted character. At one juncture, and possibly included with a certain can't-catch-him-now impudence, the camera turns to unrepentant hippie Cliff discussing the proper way to smoke the butt of a joint—called a roach in the parlance of the sixties.

The closing credits run under what to many fans has become Cliff's signature theme—the soulfully wailing "Orion."

The text on the hand-drawn video box of *Cliff 'Em All* was executed by the ubiquitous Pushead, who also created the cover's savage caricatures of the band. The idea that caricatures of a "serious" band were somehow inappropriate may have been put to rest by Aerosmith's *Draw the Line* album, on which the band was caricatured by famed *New York Times* artist Al Hirshfeld.

The designation of *Cliff 'Em All* as a *$19.98* home vid was quite intentional. Longform music videos tend to cost $24.98, but Metallica was determined to offer the most video for the least money. (Needless to say, production costs couldn't have been much lower.) There was no promotional videoclip released to music video broadcast outlets as there usually is. The producers knew it would've been an uphill battle to pursuade a video programmer to play these rather long and middling-to-poor-quality cuts. They sound horrible next to highly produced clips. Elektra *did,* however, cross-merchandise *Cliff 'Em All* with the re-released *Kill 'Em All* album.

Elektra Home Entertainment, a home video division associated with Elektra Records, released *The $19.98 Home Vid Cliff 'Em All* in April of 1988. The video sold over 25,000 copies in its first three days of release. The video was certified platinum for sales of 100,000 in its first three months on store shelves. It last appeared on the *Billboard* Top Music Videos chart in November of 1991, having racked up a total of 122 weeks on the chart.

The success of the *Cliff 'Em All* video took the band totally by surprise. They thought that a mostly bootleg-quality video—complete with unintentional camera flubs and screwing-around footage under the influence of alcohol—would be fun for the hardcore few. They were simply unaware of how many people would rather see great metal with crummy technical quality than crummy metal with great technical quality.

14

Even though no radio stations were playing Metallica, Elektra Records knew that reissuing *Kill 'Em All* would sell the album like never before. The album was re-released in January of 1988, and by July of that year sales were reported to have topped 250,000 copies.

With sales of their *first* album booming in response to an ever-growing fan base, the men of Metallica were starting to feel hard-pressed to come up with their *next* album. Writing together just hadn't been "clicking" for most of 1987, but finally, by autumn of that year, work on the next Metallica album finally started to jell.

They felt that the writing of new songs had better go a bit quicker this time, not wanting to find themselves writing at the last minute while expensive studio time ticked away (a problem, to various extents, with both *Ride the Lightning* and *Master of Puppets*).

Yet Metallica was under pressure from neither their label nor their management to hurry up and turn something in by a prefigured deadline. The administrative thinking was, These guys have always done pretty well for themselves when the world leaves them alone, so . . .

They begin with titles. "This time around we had a long list of about twenty or thirty good song titles," says James. "Slowly, when the skeleton of a song comes together and we can start feeling what sort of mood it has, we'll look over the list of titles and pick one that fits the feel of that whole thing. Then we'll talk about what ideas that song title sort of brings out, then sit down and put all the lyrics together."

There's no place for good manners when writing the new songs. As Kirk told *Guitar Player*, "Sometimes someone comes in with a part that they think is brilliant, but someone else says, 'Sorry, that won't cut it—you're overplaying.' And then you have to simplify your approach."

Metallica's songs are the product of bits and pieces of composition and improvisation that the members toss out at rehearsals or on their own. Every member puts these riffs on a riff tape. (Lars usually hums them to James, who then puts them on tape.) After careful review, the most original, catchy or just plain nasty song snippets are put onto a master riff tape. These master riffs are hammered into Metallica songs.

As a result of this riffarama approach to songwriting, the new songs were even longer than those that went before them. They were fusing one riff to another and another and another, elongating their song structure and making the trip that much longer to get back to the song's basic theme. The band was aware of how long these new tunes were running, but were unconcerned.

Tonally, the new-metal ethos ruled—scrap the old

blues-metal. Hammer away at the sharp, hard changes. When *Guitar Player* magazine suggested that new-metal bands were abandoning pentatonic (blues-oriented) scales for more diatonic ones, Kirk Hammett agreed. He considered Eric Clapton, Jeff Beck or Jimmy Page as examples of the blues-based school, and Yngwie Malmsteen a prime practitioner of the modern diatonic sound. As James would have it, long live the "psycho-sounding half-step stuff."

"When we finally sat down in mid-October and started writing, it just came together so fuckin' quickly," Lars remembers. "I was prepared for a four-month stint of songwriting, 'cause that's roughly what it took to do *Puppets*. But all of a sudden, what seemed like two days later, all the songs were written. It actually only took about nine weeks to write the songs. We started in mid-October and finished around Christmas time."

And again, the Reductive Method of Metallica took hold. "How can I put it? If you've got a piece of meat, a steak or whatever, you remove the fat and the bits of meat you don't want and what remains is a high quality steak," Lars told *Metal Hammer*. "We did the same with the songs. The result was nine songs which in comparison to the old material are more compact, thought out and mature."

Lyrically, the same principle holds true. "That's just shying away from the cliches," Lars explained to the *Washington Post*. "What else is there to say about sex and how many ways can you say it? We have nothing against sex; it's just another cliche that's easily avoidable, as is Satanism, religion, drugs or car songs."

There was a short-lived move to hire Geddy Lee of Rush to produce this next album, but the idea was soon scotched because of schedule conflicts. Lee would probably have loved to become Metallica's producer, which would have helped renew his ossifying connection to the heavy metal scene. (To the horror of some, Lars has remarked in print that more than any other band, Metallica is like Rush.)

They entered the Los Angeles studio One on One Recording on February 1, 1988. A small but well-equipped facility, One on One's control room was decorated with skin-magazine pinups, while standard junkfood-and-beer-can detritus littered its other rooms. There was also a pool table if Jason needed to get a game in.

Prior commitments had left Flemming Rasmussen unavailable until March, but the band didn't want these songs to wither on the vine. Metallica hired Mike Clink to produce this next record.

Clink had a solid reputation as a metal record producer, having worked with Guns n' Roses. He would later coproduce Megadeth's *Rust in Peace*. The GNR gang had given their seal of approval to Clink, so he took the reins—as much as any Metallica producer was allowed to.

As if they hadn't already learned their lesson, Metallica's first act, upon their return to the studio, was to start playing a new batch of old metal covers.

With Mike Clink, the band recorded the drum tracks for "Harvester of Sorrow" and "The Shortest Straw." And that was about it. The band and Mike Clink were having a lousy time trying to work together and ultimately Clink left the project. The band nevertheless felt that the time spent in the studio with Clink was not wasted in any way, and probably saved time over the entire recording process. In mid-March, Flemming Rasmussen returned to oversee production on the new album.

Once the songs were written, the Metallica studio process tended to run in this order: James and Lars would meet in the studio to play the songs. From those initial tracks, the drum tracks were recorded. After that, James would come back and lay down the rhythm guitar tracks. Then Jason's bass tracks were inserted and James would double (and sometimes even triple) the guitar tracks, adding whatever harmony parts they needed. And then finally, Kirk recorded his solos.

But in the studio, attending to all the details, it was always Lars. When recording was done, the others might disperse in all directions, but Lars would still be there to oversee the often repetitive drudgery of mixing an album.

Yet Lars has always been a genuine live-for-the-music sort, a true rock'n'roll animal who lives the rock life to its fullest. Among other things, he's been known to hoist a few too many with Guns n' Roses guitarist Slash. This was some sort of factor in the work schedule for the new album. As Lars told *Metallix*,, "You gotta take into account the Metallica lag-factor, as we call it. We definitely like to work at our own pace."

The fourth Metallica album, . . . *And Justice for All,* was their most musically ambitious and involved project to date. Whereas previous Metallica songs were built around two or three central riffs, these new songs were practically teeming with riffs. On . . . *And Justice for All*, the riffs sang, soared, sighed, cried out, shrieked and choked on their own bile. Riffs were bashed, thrashed, shaped, sculpted and transformed into towering, breathtaking cities of sound.

The album begins with "Blackened," a bleak portrait of the burned-out planet left over from an environmental holocaust. Amid the pounding beats, a beautiful, tangled melody is taken over by a pirouetting solo, and guitar twins and triplets sail upwards from the ugly morass.

"Blackened" posed special problems for Kirk, as it has three tempo changes. Kirk's intricate solo had to glide smoothly over all of them.

The album's name was taken from Norman Jewison's 1979 satirical movie ... *And Justice for All,* which impressed James with its themes of a sick judicial system. The title song echoes the film, with its savage take on hypocrisy and corruption in the courts. Its pretty, classically inflected theme is unceremoniously stomped on as "... And Justice for All" turns into a wild gallery of shuddering riffs, topped off by a symphonic guitar chorus.

A strident and probing defense of freedom of choice, "Eye of the Beholder" marches its metal guitars in military-riff formation across the scorched terrain of ominous, monster-movie chords. "What do you think is art? What's pornography? What's disgusting? What's brilliant? Just what's in your head," James told *Circus.*

"Eye of the Beholder" was written in response to the Jello Biafra obscenity case in the mid-eighties. Jello Biafra (born Eric Boucher) was the leader and singer for San Francisco punk mainstays the Dead Kennedys. He was charged with distributing harmful matter to minors, because of the 1985 Dead Kennedys album *Frankenchrist.* The album contained a poster by noted pop surrealist H. R. Giger, who designed much of the landmark science fiction film *Alien.* The poster depicted an array of disembodied phalluses poised to enter an opposite array of orifices. One California teenager bought the album, and when that teenager's mother saw the poster, she filed an official complaint. Jello Biafra faced a maximum penalty of one year in jail or a $2,000 fine. The case ended in a hung jury and there was no second trial. Ultimately, the legal money-drain this case put on Jello Biafra wiped out his record label, Alternative Tentacles, and broke up the Dead Kennedys.

As James told *Circus* about cases like these, "You can't really express yourself the way you want. It's kinda scary. I mean, you've got a choice—if you don't want to look at it, don't look at it."

Another song on the theme of encroached freedoms is "The Shortest Straw," a meditation on the witch-hunting and ostracism of those that society finds "different." Without having written any music yet, the band was toying with the song title "The Shortest Straw." They were intrigued by a member of a supposedly equal society who drew "the shortest straw" and would become a pariah. Q Prime manager Cliff Burnstein suggested they read *Naming Names,* by author and editor Victor Navasky. A chronicle of coercion and betrayal in the McCarthy era, *Naming Names* gave the band a focal point for their vision of the social outcast.

"Harvester of Sorrow" is an all-out, high-powered evil-personified horror show in the classic traditions of "No Remorse" or "The Four Horsemen." As a Middle Eastern funk-metal groove shoves the song forward, overlapping call-and-response voices suggest echoes from the labyrinths of hell.

Like most of the *Justice* song, "Harvester" is reasonably long and contains distinct parts. A 1992-released EP featured a live version of the song. The band wrote in the liner notes that they'd played that song "about 275 times before." And yet, before that crowd in Graz, Austria, they managed to leave out the entire second chorus.

Clearly, the album's masterpiece is "One," a searing antiwar portrait of a maimed, bedridden soldier, trapped in a living death. The song opens with sounds of machine guns and soldiers under fire. Then settling over the battlefield is a delicate acoustic theme—James's measured, restrained vocals speaking of a man who can't move an inch. Majestic guitars ultimately form a bridge to the pummeling riffs of the song's final section. With instrumentation that follows the song's lyrical theme, a peaceful beginning suggests the peace of the dead, but the frenzy that follows shows that there's something more going on under the surface.

Whether the song grew out of a serious consideration of the plight of the handicapped or the details of an utter gross-out, the band had been speculating on what life would be like for someone with no means of movement—with both of his legs and both of his arms amputated. But what if this person is also deprived of all senses? To be, as Lars put it, a " 'living brain' type of thing?" As the more profound ramifications of the dire gross-out started appearing to the band, manager Cliff Burnstein suggested they check out *Johnny Got His Gun* by Dalton Trumbo. Its protagonist, Joe Bonham, is left maimed in such a way.

A narrative from the borders of madness, "The Frayed

Lars in Moscow at Tushino. *Courtesy Novosti-Sipa.*

Ends of Sanity" begins with a martial beat accompanied by the universally recognized *Wizard of Oz* chant. This amusing digression is topped off by an angry, grinding riff that snarls and strains on a short leash.

Cliff Burton gets a composer's credit for "To Live Is to Die," as the song uses four of his lines found after his death. Essentially a Cliff-styled instrumental, "To Live Is to Die" begins with an acoustic folk theme, lost when a monster riff comes in to rule the song. A cleverly wrought Metallica mini-symphony, a second acoustic stretch is matched with evocative, simulated cello sounds. There were about fifteen separate guitar tracks in the mix.

The song also features one of the least diatonic—and most blues-drenched—solos that Kirk Hammett has ever put on record. The recording of this song was finished at five A.M., just before the band was due to leave for their first Monsters of Rock tour.

"Dyer's Eve," a child's rebellion against his sheltered life, was triggered by James's reflections on his own youth. As Christian Scientists, the elder Hetfields loved talking about people who—according to their Christian Scientist beliefs—had been cured of disease without the aid of medicine. One daughter of a Christian Science family had broken her arm, and all the adults marveled at how well she was doing now that her arm had gotten better without medicine. All James can remember about her arm was that it was clearly *not* all right: the girl definitely did not have full use of the mangled-looking arm.

As for the song's title, Lars recalled the 1970 film *Little Big Man*, in which Dustin Hoffman's "grandfather" (Chief Dan George) says that a certain day is "a good day for dying." Lars has likened "Dyer's Eve" to that concept—a "Dyer's Eve" would be a good night for dying. But, as Lars told *Creem Metal*, "It's not a real word so I guess you can send the dictionary police after us. We're corrupting the minds of young Americans."

As for those cover versions that the band started playing as soon as they walked in the studio, two of those were recorded as well. A Budgie tune from 1983, "Breadfan" creates a metal fusillade of bludgeoning guitars. A slow middle section is then overwhelmed by the return of the main monster boogie-cruncher riff. Also recorded was Diamond Head's "The Prince," another cover marked by righteous, rapid-fire riffing.

When the album was done, . . . And Justice for All contained nearly sixty-five minutes of music. While that much music is easily contained on one compact disc, it would've been just about impossible to fit it on one vinyl album. It was suggested that by merely removing one song it could be released as a single album, but the band felt that they had to trust their instincts. Although the vinyl album was becoming less and less important to the music industry in the advent of the CD, the group insisted that the album be released as a double-LP set. This idea had additional advantages. In the mastering process, an album with less music allows for deeper grooves to be cut into the vinyl. Deeper grooves make for a lot less extraneous noise.

Both *Justice* and *Master of Puppets* used the mastering process called Direct Metal Mastering (DMM). Most album masters are cut with a lathe into a lacquer-coated aluminum disc, which then undergoes several other treatments before it can be used to start pressing albums. The DMM method, however, cuts the master not into lacquer, but rather into a copper disc, which saves a couple of steps—and some sound quality—on the way to the pressing plant. All these improvements in recording quality mean one thing: the music can be played *louder*.

With this album came another event: For the first time in Metallica history, the band released a real-live single. (After all, singles were for bands that got their songs on the radio.) "One" and "Eye of the Beholder" both came out in the rapidly disappearing seven-inch vinyl format. However, there were still no plans to shoot a promotional videoclip.

. . . *And Justice For All* was released on September 2, 1988, to general critical praise. It evoked comparisons that no other thrash band had ever gotten before. Some writers likened *Justice* to the work of Yes during their seventies prog-rock years. Lars couldn't disagree. Whatever the critics decided, . . . *And Justice For All* had been judged a winner.

"It's too easy to say something like, 'Yeah, we don't care if the album doesn't sell one copy or 10,000 or 10 million,'" Lars remarked to *Hit Parader*. "Anyone who tells you that—deep down, they're not telling you the truth. But, at the end of the day the thing that matters is that you make a record that's completely yours from beginning to end—with no sacrifices, no compromises, no corners cut. You have to feel good about it."

15

> "Every tour has to
> have a scapegoat
> and Kingdom Come
> are the ones for the
> Monsters."
>
> —Lars Ulrich on general
> feelings directed towards
> Kingdom Come
> (*Faces Rocks*)

The typical American concert experience allows for two—or rarely—three bands at one show. Periodically, larger festivals are held, but generally as a one-shot, one-location deal. In Europe, there is a far greater tradition of these multiband, traveling festivals. One was called the Monsters of Rock.

In 1988, Van Halen manager Ed Leffler became the driving force behind the first American Monsters of Rock tour. With a roster of at least four bands, Leffler estimated that it would require a retinue of twenty-five trucks (as well as buses and airplanes), two different lighting crews, two different sound crews and three separate stages. He even hired two different accountants to keep track of it all.

Featuring Van Halen, the Scorpions, Metallica, Dokken and Kingdom Come, the Monsters of Rock had a ten-week, twenty-three-city itinerary. But the tour had no guarantee of success. Around the country simultaneous tours were being played by Def Leppard, Whitesnake, Judas Priest, Ozzy Osbourne, AC/DC and Iron Maiden. This superabundance of on-the-road metal was bound to cut into everyone's ticket sales.

As Q Prime's Cliff Burnstein told the *Los Angeles Times,* "The competition is going to be murderous out there."

Yet as plans for the Monsters tour proceeded, Metallica was still working frantically at One on One to finish ... *And Justice for All.* It was a last-minute, down-to-the-wire gesture, but by the fourth week in May 1988, they were done. (Well, not exactly, but close enough.)

Before jumping right into a major national stadium tour, the band thought it wise to give themselves a little warm-up. On the nights of May 23 and 24, Metallica returned to the Los Angeles rock club the Troubadour, appearing as the Frayed Ends. The gigs were unannounced to the press, but the band had already alerted its L.A.-area fan club members through a direct mailing. Despite the band's low profile, the shows were met by a line stretching around the block on Santa Monica Boulevard. "Frayed Ends" had fooled no one.

"We hadn't played in front of people in nine months," Lars recalled. "It was fun! The place was about the size of my fuckin' bathroom. We once opened for Ratt there!" Lars's enthusiasm was exceptional—the band had been up all night at One on One just before the gig. Other "secret gigs" the band played at around this time included shows at New York's Cat Club as well as clubs in Washington, D.C. The same fan club arrangements were in effect as at the Troubadour.

With the last-minute studio frenzy and the rowdiness of the Troubadour gigs behind them, Metallica traveled to the verdant surroundings of East Troy, Wisconsin. The Monster of Rock tour started there on May 27, at the Alpine Valley Music Theatre in front of forty thousand fans who banged their collective head in appreciation.

With five years of festival gigs under his belt, Lars thought that stadium shows like these were a fifty-fifty venture—either the bands would come off great or the whole thing would sink like a lead canoe. Lars was, however, pleased that each band on the Monsters tour was allotted about an hour—as opposed to the ridiculously short four- or five-song sets accorded other nonheadlining acts. Nevertheless, despite their generous set length, Metallica played next to no material from the just-completed *Justice,* preferring to stick to the hits that were sure to be requested.

When Metallica hit the road, they were as well organized as Boy Scouts. They came equipped with a first aid kit, toothpaste, foot powder, hangover cures, stomach medicines, toothbrush holders and traveling soap dishes (each with a band member's name written on it in Magic Marker). By now, touring was no haphazard thing.

One medical situation that Metallica couldn't have prepared for was the discovery of Lars Ulrich's tinnitus, an ear affliction brought about by prolonged exposure to loud noise. Tinnitus sufferers experience ringing in the ears, usually accompanied by a marked loss of hearing. Rockers of all stripes are said to have come down with the condition— from Pete Townshend of the Who to Clint Conley of the avant-punk band Mission of Burma. From the Monsters of Rock tour onwards, Lars would wear the earplugs throughout. Although he first felt a bit wimpish about having to wear the earplugs, examples of other musicians whose hearing was completely lost brought him back to practicality. Lars would keep James on his monitor because he found him easier to follow than Kirk or Jason.

Often, Metallica felt that they were the underdogs on the MOR. They were noticeably lacking for a heavy stage-show extravaganza, and they were never likely to break out of their T-shirt and jeans wardrobe. Yet they clearly preferred the role of the underdog, enjoying their mangy-little-brother status with regard to the other bands. Underdog or not, though, Metallica could rest assured that every MOR crowd would contain a strong contingent of Metallica fans.

The mixing for . . . *And Justice for All* was completed after Metallica had hit the road with the Monsters of Rock tour. Wherever in the country Lars and James might be, they'd hop in a plane and make their way to rural Bearsville, New York, to continue the sometimes agonizing task of mixing their record. Viewing the beautiful wooded area that surrounded the studio, Lars felt a sharp contrast to the thousands of screaming fans he'd faced a day before.

The mixing engineers hired for . . . *And Justice for All* were Steve Thomson and Michael Barbiero. The Metallica members thought that Thompson-and-Barbiero-mixed albums by Guns n' Roses, Tesla and Dokken were evidence that Thompson and Barbiero wouldn't alter the sound the band wanted.

In a certain regard, allowing Metallica to play a festival gig with a classic metal band became a bit of a high-decibel autograph book for the band. Each true "Monster" of rock that Metallica played with was duly noted by the band members. They had been previously honored to play with such living legends as Deep Purple and ZZ Top. Metallica had never toured with any of these Monsters of Rock bands before.

Touring with Van Halen was another step for the meet-the-rock-gods scrapbook. Lars commented that no matter what the critics and public may think of a David Lee Roth—less Van Halen, they were still a highly influential and legendary band. (An assessment that could never be made without considering Eddie Van Halen's transcendent guitar playing.) By this time, Lars felt that the only highly influential band with whom they *hadn't* shared a bill was Iron Maiden. As Lars remarked to *Creem Metal,* "To see a band like Metallica on a poster that said Deep Purple and then Dio and then Metallica—which happened last year—is great. It was a huge moment."

Many felt that the diversity among the metal styles on the MOR tour would discourage some fans, but this didn't prove true. "The line-up they put together is pretty fuckin' cool," he told *Circus,* "because all the groups are different from each other to some extent. I know we're the most left-field, but it's not like if you close your eyes, you'll be confused as to what band is on."

If any of the Metallica members had ever idolized the Scorpions, their affection may not have survived the Monsters tour. Kirk recalled how disappointed he was that the Scorpions seemed to put on the *exact same* show for every single gig—with identical stage moves. An upbeat Jason tried to keep from slagging them, but also agreed that rock'n'roll seemed to be an act to them. An act that had to be kept up at all times—even at breakfast in an airport snack bar.

But the worst-received band on the MOR tour were Euro-rockers Kingdom Come. Given a strong major-label push in the U.S. during 1988, their slavish imitation of Led Zeppelin led the critics—and most audiences—to dismiss them out of hand.

Fans who actually *liked* the bands ended up in a near riot at a Sunday afternoon Monsters show at the Los Angeles Coliseum.

Metallica had just started its three P.M. set when hyper-enthusiastic fans broke through the fencing that separated the stage from the stands and ran towards the already-thrashing Metallica. Lots of chairs were thrown, and one narrowly missed a band member.

The show was stopped briefly—ostensibly because of a power failure—but the Coliseum staff used the time to quickly pick up all of the tossed chairs by the stage. Metallica's set was allowed to resume. Later on, during a subsequent set, plastic cups of soda and firecrackers were tossed from the upper seats, but there was no further trouble.

Police estimated that thousands of fans had descended on the field. Although the Coliseum show represented an isolated incident of brainless vandalism rather than rampant youth violence, Brian Murphy, president of promoter Avalon Attractions, felt that the venue may not really have been suited to hard-rock shows. A representative from the Coliseum itself also suggested that heavy metal shows might be ruled out in the future. Again, the actions of the asinine metal minority were bringing down the wrath of the Powers That Be on everybody.

After two and a half months on the road, the Monsters of Rock tour ground to a halt in Denver, Colorado. The MOR was seen as a savvy, influence-expanding move on the part of Metallica. Fans who had come to see the Scorpions, Dokken and Van Halen had seen Metallica and had been impressed. Even Van Halen had been impressed. VH lead singer and lifelong metal marauder Sammy Hagar was a bona fide Metallica fan by tour's end, telling *Hit Parader*, "They'll be the new kings of rock, just you wait and see."

16

That Metallica would never make a rock video was an eternal given—on the same order of certainty as *The New York Times* never running funnies or the Chicago Cubs never winning the Series. The question of music videos would inevitably come up in interviews, and the band was always quick to put it down. On one occasion, when Lars was making disparaging remarks about MTV's metal show *Headbanger's Ball,* he repeated that the band had no intention of making a video.

They'd always spurned rock videoclips, as they were clichéd and tended to turn the most impressive rock'n'roller in to a pathetic, posturing, lip-synching laughingstock. But after making the *Justice* album, there were thoughts in the air about an original, thoroughly Metallicized videoclip. With the convention-smashing success of *Cliff 'Em All* they thought that perhaps the dreaded "rock video" could be an enjoyable thing to watch. Lars had always said that the band wasn't making a video. But he was usually careful to add that the idea had never been ruled out either.

When Metallica agreed to make a videoclip for "One," they were sure to leave no escape hatch unlocked. The band reached an agreement with Elektra that if they didn't like how the video came out, the clip would be shelved and they'd be under no obligation to make another.

Since the primary source for "One" was Dalton Trumbo's novel *Johnny Got His Gun,* a call went out for its 1971 movie version—directed by Trumbo himself.

A Hollywood screenwriter from the late thirties on, Dalton Trumbo had worked on a number of film classics, including *Kitty Foyle, Spartacus* and *Thirty Seconds Over Tokyo.*

Johnny Got His Gun was written in 1939, when World War II was flaring up all over the world—but wouldn't ensnare America for another two years. At first the novel was a favorite of the antiwar, workers-of-the-world-unite left. Then, when the U.S. joined the war, right-wing extremists who wanted to keep us from war with Hitler tried to spread the book's antiwar message. This was rather unsettling to Trumbo, who was a member of the Communist party in the 1940s.

Called before the House Committee on Un-American Activities, he refused to answer its questions and was sent to jail. As one of the so-called Hollywood Ten, Trumbo was blacklisted from working in Hollywood.

Trumbo continued to work, though, writing under other names. He won a 1956 Academy Award for his original story of *The Brave One,* which was written under the name Robert Rich. In 1960, director Otto Preminger defied the blacklist by publicly announcing Trumbo as the writer of *Exodus.* (In his "Talkin' John Birch Society Blues," Bob

Dylan remarks that the notorious American Nazi George Lincoln Rockwell picketed the movie *Exodus*. Trumbo's official reemergence in the film world was probably one reason.)

When the Vietnam War was tearing America apart in the late 1960s and early '70s, *Johnny Got His Gun* became required reading for young men petrified of going to war. Its antiwar horror reinforced the fear and distrust draft-age young men felt toward their government. Such a sixties staple was *Johnny Got His Gun* that the cover of versions sold today still shows a silhouetted hand making the Vietnam-era peace sign.

There seemed to be only two prints of the movie still in existence. The first was owned by the estate of Dalton Trumbo, who died in 1976, and the second was located in Italy. After some negotiations, the Italians released a video copy of the movie.

Metallica and management screened *Johnny Got His Gun,* and picked out their favorite scenes and lines. They wanted clips from the movie to play a prominent role in the video.

A few well-known rock video directors were asked to shoot the band footage that would accompany the movie scenes. All turned Metallica down. Fortunately, a less-known but highly talented video director *was* available: Michael Salomon. "I think, at the time, there wasn't that much interest amongst big directors to get involved with Metallica," he recalls. "I don't know why. I guess maybe because they were a fringe group at that point.... Maybe the band wanted to use people that were not necessarily out of the heavy metal genre."

Michael Salomon, who'd directed clips by such country artists as Sawyer Brown, Dolly Parton, Glen Campbell and

Buck Owens, was not known for his work on heavy metal videos. Salomon worked with noted director Wayne Isham as an editor, then as a free-lance editor for the major vid-clip production house O Pictures.

It was O Pictures that approached Michael Salomon to codirect the "One" clip, along with Bill Pope. Pope, who leaned towards the more visually oriented job of director of photography, would shoot the black-and-white footage of the band lip-synching the song in an abandoned Los Angeles warehouse.

Michael Salomon's job was this: to use crucial snippets of the movie *Johnny Got His Gun* to convey its plot, while not cramming so much dialogue into the "One" mix that the actual song would be completely buried.

The film, which alternates in time between present-day scenes in black-and-white and flashbacks in color, was badly washed out. The color scenes were just barely recognizable as such. "I imagine at one point it was very apparent that one was really vivid color and one was black and white," Michael Salomon comments, "but the print was so bad. It was very washed, and you can almost not tell." They'd asked the Italian film-owners to boost the colors as much as possible when the film was copied. The results were less than overwhelming, and the tape lost yet another generation of quality when it was converted from the European PAL format to American NTSC.

"I think they brought me in just to give the whole thing shape," explains Michael Salomon. "They realized that it was basically an editorial job, because they wanted to incorporate so much of the movie. They probably saw it as a logistical nightmare that they could just dump in my lap and I'd take the ball from that point on."

Beginning a couple weeks before the band would go before the cameras in a gray-looking warehouse, Salomon was given a copy of "One" and a substandard copy of *Johnny Got His Gun*. In a sound studio, he married the right plot-conveying soundbytes to the song.

Salomon played his audio-only version of movie dialogue and Metallica song blended together. "I had to have them imagine that there would be visuals that would go with it," he remembers. "And I would say that probably ninety-five percent of it stayed that way from that initial meeting. I think the band was a little taken aback by how much of the movie I put in there. It's a very complicated story and to do it with just one or two soundbytes here and there really wouldn't have made it. Basically, every time there was an extended guitar intro or guitar solo or anything like that, I covered the whole thing up. The musician side of them said 'That's not cool, we don't get to hear the music.' But I think they realized that for this particular clip, the story element was more important. Plus, everybody knew that there was gonna be another version released that was just a performance clip."

Michael Salomon finished editing both audio and video segments of the "One" clip at Post Logic in L.A. The whole process had taken three weeks.

Although Michael Salomon may have been able to convince Metallica that there should be movie dialogue all over their song, he couldn't cheat the shots. When video directors "cheat" a shot, they show a performer playing an instrument, but don't worry about having the music match the visual. When occasional shot-cheater Salomon tried it with Metallica, the band insisted that the pictures and the music match perfectly.

The "One" video begins with statue-still images of James, followed immediately by the explosion that sets in motion the film's horrible chain of events. James, Jason and Kirk are shown torso-only, the frame cutting off their heads and legs. Against these rich-toned black-and-white images of Metallica are superimposed a series of moments from *Johnny Got His Gun*. Against the moving acoustic-guitar theme of "One" are shown poignant scenes from the film— the stark, hellish images of the bedridden protagonist and the nurse who tends to his mutilated body. Cutaways to the band become more and more furious as "One" reaches its clamorous conclusion—but on a completely unexpected note. At the song's abrupt cutoff, the soundtrack takes over and concludes the video with a hospital chorus singing "Keep the Homefires Burning."

While artfully conveying the themes of *Johnny Got His Gun* in a pastiche of taut, visceral moments, the video seems to leave up in the air the fate of the helpless protagonist Joe Bonham. The original novel of *Johnny Got His Gun* ended on a horrible note of certainty that Joe would remain in his pathetic state forever. In the videoclip, there's a strong sense that the sympathetic nurse provided a risky death-with-dignity deliverance for Joe.

"It's a little vague in the clip, but actually there's the general who's ordered the doctors to keep him alive when he's supposedly being killed," Michael Salomon explains. "He walks in at the last second. It's not real clear, and it was left ambiguous like that. In fact, he *is* alive at the very end. You *do* hear him talking at the end of the clip, he keeps saying, *'I'll never get out of here, help me.'* So you know that he's still alive. At least in my mind, at least in the minds of all the people that viewed it. But maybe it was because we knew what the ending was and it was more clear to us, since we knew what it was supposed to be."

The question was this: Would the *music video outlets* know what the "One" videoclip was supposed to be? Cliff

Burnstein would tell of a former MTV executive who said that the only place Metallica was going to be seen on MTV was on its news show.

On January 22, 1989, the "One" clip made its debut on the *Headbanger's Ball*. The MTV veejays promoted the clip heavily during the preceding afternoon's *Top 15 Countdown*. The clip came in number 13 in requests—even before it had been aired. After it had been aired, it went to number 1. MTV's "Smash or Trash" segment tallied up thirty thousand calls for the "One" video. It was the biggest "Smash or Trash" response ever, 78 percent were in favor of the video.

With this introduction, the video was moved into late-night and overnight time slots—most often the domain of esoteric videos. But still the requests kept coming in, and soon the video was being shown in the afternoon. Finally, it hit number 1 on MTV's video countdown. The video ultimately reached heavy rotation, MTV's category for the most-seen videos. Metal bands didn't usually reach this level of exposure.

Other, lesser-known music video broadcasters were having similar experiences with the clip. "One" went to number 1 at Tampa, Florida, video station V32, and became a top-5 request at Hit Video USA, which—with a preponderance of pop and urban music—had a format even less hospitable to metal than MTV's.

The folks at Elektra told the band that they thought they could get "One" played on the radio, but that they'd need to cut a couple minutes out of it. The band didn't think it constituted any sort of breach of faith to release a radio edit of "One," so the edit was authorized.

"We did an edit of 'For Whom the Bell Tolls' five years ago and no one cared," Lars remarked to *Circus*. "Now, 'cause we've sold so many more albums, there's always someone whining about something you do. Who cares? If it turns more people on to Metallica, it's okay."

An edited video version was the counterpart to an edited audio version, and it consisted simply of the band's warehouse shots. It contained no sound or images from *Johnny Got His Gun*. Needless to say, the lip-synched edited version bore a certain resemblance to the kind of let's-pretend-to-sing-and-play-our-instruments conventions that turned the band off the music video in the first place. How could they commit the cardinal sin of—shades of Milli Vanilli—lip-synching?

"They never really objected to it," Michael Salomon remembers. "I think they were trusting in that they would hold off their judgment until they saw the piece finally with all the visuals in it. I think by that point, which was already three or four weeks later, they had already gotten used to the idea."

After the example of the *Cliff 'Em All* video, Elektra Home Entertainment probably guessed that the uncounted multitudes of Metallica fans would buy a reasonably low-priced home video version of "One." Produced by Sharon Oreck and Anita Wetterstedt for O Pictures, the home video release *2 of One* features the full-length and the edited versions of the clip. Opening the tape is an interview with Lars, conducted by an unseen Len Epand of music video house Flashframe.

The success of the "One" clip is believed to be responsible for the single's high chart numbers, hitting number 35 on *Billboard*'s "Hot 100" singles chart on April 8, 1989, after two months on the chart. A learning experience with a Top 40 payoff—this first video couldn't have been such a trial.

Jason bringing metal to Moscow. *Courtesy Novosti-Sipa.*

As Lars told *Metal Edge,* "The video proved to us that things we thought of as evil aren't as evil as we thought—as long as we do it our way."

Metallica performed "One" on the Thirty-first Annual Grammy Awards show, broadcast from L.A.'s Shrine Auditorium, February 22, 1989. The group was nominated for a "coveted" Grammmy in the category of best hard-rock/metal performance, vocal or instrumental for . . . *And Justice for All.* The other contenders included AC/DC's *Blow Up Your Video,* Iggy Pop's *Cold Metal,* Jane's Addiction's *Nothing's Shocking* and Jethro Tull's *Crest of a Knave.* Jethro Tull won the Grammy, sending waves of incredulity throughout the metal world.

Lars thought that Metallica's appearance on a show like the Grammy awards might elevate the position of metal among the disapproving multitudes. As he told the *Washington Post,* "We didn't come out and perform Satanic rituals on stage or rape girls, and from our point of view it was a good song."

The following year, at the Thirty-second Annual Grammy broadcast, the single *One* was nominated for best metal performance, vocal or instrumental, against Dokken's *Beast from the East,* Queensrÿche's *I Don't Believe in Love,* Faith No More's *The Real Thing,* and Soundgarten's *Ultramega O.K.* This time, Metallica won. The band that had to scrape up $50 to get their first song bumped up to a reel-to-reel tape had brought home its first Grammy.

17

> **"I remember back when I stood for three hours waiting for autographs, and when the star just hopped in his limo and took off, I'd think, 'You dick, I hate you.' I'd go home, rip down his posters . . ."**
>
> —James Hetfield on rock stars' traditional relationship to their fans (*Rolling Stone*)

When the Monsters of Rock tour ended, Metallica took about a five-minute breather and launched into their first arenas-only road trip, the 1988–89 Damaged Justice tour. The first such tour for any new-metal band, Damaged Justice would feature Metallica's most elaborate stage show, which tied in visually with the socially conscious . . . *And Justice for All*.

For reasons best known to the band, management and promoters, Damaged Justice kicked off on September 10, 1988, in the still-fully-Communist Yugoslavia. After shows before wildly grateful Eastern bloc metalheads, the tour went on through England, the Scandinavian countries, France, Italy and Germany. This first leg would bring the band to the capital cities of Europe for two months. Previously, Metallica hadn't had a Euro-gig since the '87 Castle Donington show. Although the European segment of Damaged Justice ended on November 5, the entire journey would encompass more concerts and mileage then anyone yet realized.

Of all European countries, Lars remembered Poland as the most exciting, with the highest level of energizing metal mania anywhere. The kids in Poland just seemed *involved*. And indeed Poland had been the cosmopolitan and West-ward-looking of the often drab Warsaw Pact nations.

Of course, capitalism won out in Poland, and the pressures of capitalism rule the day on any rock'n'roll tour. One German show was a case in point. Metallica tour manager Bobby Schneider saw a concertgoer illegally snapping picures with a professional-looking set. As this sort of free-lancing drives legitimate rock photographers nuts, Schneider waded out into the crowd to stop the surreptitious shutterbug. From the stage, a laughing James Hetfield told the photographer that he'd been nailed. Schneider tried to grab the man by the scruff of the neck, but his hair—actually a wig—came off in Schneider's hands instead. It became one of James's favorite entertain-ments of the entire tour.

Before the start of a concert, the venue sound system would blast "Ecstasy of Gòld," a song from *The Good, the Bad, and the Ugly* soundtrack, before the group took the stage. A monument to overblown, melodramatic sound-track music everywhere, this perfectly ponderous Ennio Morricone theme serves as self-parody, to deflate the thun-der-and-brimstone pretentions that plague heavy metal.

While performing in politically divided Belfast, Northern Ireland, Metallica stayed in the Europa Hotel, which had the distinction of being the most often bombed of any hotel in Europe. The Europa had withstood twenty-nine actual bombings, which explained why the matches the band found in their hotel room ashtrays had the inscription WE'RE

BACK. The Metallica crew found this about as reassuring as the razor-wire-topped fences that surrounded the hotel and the security checkpoint at the entrance. This was not the sort of "getting bombed" to which Metallica was generally accustomed.

Backstage at their October 1 show at Belfast's Antrim Forum, a British soldier walked his explosives-sniffing German shepherd to and fro. Very much aware of the sectarian violence in that region, Lars remembers feeling a bit uneasy whenever the flash pots exploded during "One."

On the Justice tour, the sheer force of cranked-up Metallica could blow away more than just the audience. Onstage, Kirk felt a nearly physical force from the torrent of sounds flying from their massive PAs. He told *People*, "The adrenaline goes so fast my eyes bulge. I can hardly stand up anymore." Lars has commented that the decibel peak onstage at a Metallica show was 126—a volume he likens to sitting inside a 747 jet engine as it takes off. In fact, readings of 127 decibels have been taken by some fans.

Band and crew traveled through Europe in traditional style, on a VCR-equipped tourbus where action, horror and most importantly, Clint Eastwood spaghetti westerns are shown. (With soundtracks by Ennio Morricone, naturally.) Metallica's swill-of-choice remained Jägermeister throughout the Damaged Justice tour, although the band was beginning to downplay its legendary rowdiness. "When we started touring we did have three or four years of every excess known to man," James told *Musician*, adding, "Bottles of vodka every day; if it had a pulse, fuck it. It's great, but after a while it becomes less fun." James also notes, almost proudly, that he was crawling around his hotel hallway in the nude recently, and had thrown up on a telephone a couple days before that. Clearly, Metallica hadn't transformed themselves into followers of the take-good-care-of-your-body-and-it'll-take-good-care-of-you philosophy.

"When we're on the road, there's always something that hurts," Lars told *Hit Parader.* "Maybe it's your hand from getting blisters or your head from drinking too much the day before. But it's really not that bad."

Aside from intramural tomfoolery, the physical act of playing can be as physically taxing as any athletic regimen. One solution: solos. "The main reason we have a bass solo and a guitar solo in our show is to give the other guys a chance to rest," Kirk explained to *Guitar Player.* "When the energy level isn't at its peak, it shows. When you're tired, the meter goes all over the place and the playing gets sloppy."

To the hundreds of thousands of raging metal men and women who saw Metallica on Damaged Justice, there was no sloppiness apparent. James Hetfield's Ernie Ball guitar strings sang poignantly during "Blackened" and stung like needles on "Seek and Destroy." Diamond Head cover "Helpless" and Budgie cover "Breadfan" surfaced during this tour, as did oldies "Whiplash" and "The Four Horsemen." Songs such as ". . . And Justice for All" and "To Live Is to Die" would be performed on this tour, proba-bly for the last time.

The most striking feature of the Damaged Justice stage was the crumbling figure of blind Justice, a figure that adorns the album cover to . . . *And Justice for All.* Nick-named Doris by the band, the statue was built piece by (numbered) piece during the concert, only to be "blown apart" before the encores begin. An explosion sounded as each part of Doris flew off. Ropes attached to the Doris parts kept them from flying off into the audience.

Besides doing their best to keep statue segments from falling on their heads, the Metallicans have always been one of the most fan-accommodating bands of all time. When the kids gathered outside the backstage entrance for autographs, the band let them inside—in groups of ten to twelve or so. Waiting inside, they oblige the crowd to get autographs, take pictures, or have a brief chat. The band would spend over an hour doing this after every show. As Lars commented to *Metal Shop,* "I think it's pretty easy to see that we're not businessmen disguised as musicians who put on wigs and pretend the music we're playing is so great. Then when the show is over, you're somebody else. That's not us."

The band has also stood up for its fans on occasion, especially regarding the inalienable Right to Mosh. Lars has agreed that there may be a little physical contact in front of the stage, and even a couple kids who get led off by security, but the vast majority at Metallica shows keep pretty cool.

"There are certain tensions and frustrations that build up in a lot of kids from day-to-day dealings with the bullshit of school or work or whatever," Lars continued to *Metal Shop.* "When they finally come out to these kinds of shows, it's a way of them releasing those energies. And that can be quite manic or rough or raw and energized."

No one ever fell asleep at a Damaged Justice show— just the sight of Lars smashing his Zildjians on "Harvester of Sorrow" or the sound of Jason's driving five-string bass lines on the punk cover "The Last Caress" could get an arena of fans howling like wolves. And if anyone needed a break from the two and a half hour show, the lobby concessions would offer nineteen different T-shirt designs during the tour.

The second wind of Damaged Justice blew Metallica into Toledo, Ohio, on November 15, 1988. It was the first of thirty U.S. dates, each playing to crowds of ten thousand or more.

When Metallica returned to its spawning ground, the L.A. area, there was another pointless incident that would besmirch the name of heavy metal before the establishment media.

On the first night of Metallica's Long Beach Arena shows, rowdy fans destroyed around three thousand seats. "There was no violence, no one got hurt, but three thousand seats died," a perplexed Lars recalled to the *Washington Post.* "It's hard to understand why someone goes, 'Gee, I love this band, I'm going to kill my seat.' I don't quite understand the connection."

Since there was another show scheduled for the following night, Lars went on local radio and told the fans that whatever they are releasing their hostilities against, it all ends up directed back at Metallica, because the band would have to pay for the damage. There was little vandalism thereafter, and little on the rest of the tour.

When the American leg of the tour had run its course, Metallica flew overseas for an itinerary of shows in Japan, Australia, New Zealand, Hong Kong and Thailand. These dates had resulted from the management's honoring the band's requests to schedule some exotic, off-the-beaten-touring-circuit cities.

Although the enthusiasm of the Japanese is legendary, there are still distinct differences in the audiences from one city to the next. The Tokyo crowd was a typically rowdy metal mob, yet the fans in such cities as Osaka and Nagoya were eerily restrained. James was sorely tempted to make I-can-hear-a-pin-drop jokes to these audiences—and on at least one occasion, did.

After Asia, Metallica couldn't stay away from the good ol' USA, and played newly scheduled dates across the country. After that, Metallica played Brazil, and then returned to the tour's starting point, Europe, for another three weeks of dates. When the crew packed up Doris for the last time, Metallica had been on the road for nineteen months—and a staggering 270 performances.

As a wearied Kirk Hammett told *Metallix,* "I have a new house I haven't seen yet, a new car I haven't seen yet, and I miss eating food that my wife has cooked for me."

18

"He's known for producing a lot of these wimpy pop metal bands and now he just made the transition to a wimpy thrash metal band."

—Kirk Hammett on the hiring of Bob Rock (*Loud*)

When Metallica was barnstorming the hemispheres on the Damaged Justice tour, Kirk started noticing something when he looked out at that sea of Metallicized faces. As he told *Rolling Stone,* "Everyone would have these *long* faces. And I'd think, 'Goddamn, they're not enjoying it as much as we are.'" Ultimately, every member of Metallica had felt borne down under the weight of those leaden riffs running over and over. Although it made sense in the studio, some of these songs were too long for their own good in concert. And it was ". . . And Justice for All" that proved to be the most wearying of them all.

When Metallica sat down in the summer of 1990 to write the songs that would ultimately become *Metallica,* they were determined not to write another batch like those on *Justice.* Although they didn't wholly disown the album, they began to see it as more a learning experience than a masterpiece. (Fans would certainly recognize it as both.)

"It was a challenge for us to jam every fucking riff in the universe into one song and make it work," James told

Rolling Stone. "Now we're pretty much doing the opposite. Which is even more of a challenge."

Kirk saw the new approach the band was looking for as a way of getting back to basic musical ideas and song structures, allowing him more flexibility as a guitarist and James more flexibility as a vocalist.

For Lars's part, he started taking more notice of the "non-European" metal and hard rock. Instead of the precise Euro-rockers he'd usually favor, Lars began rediscovering the hearty, blues-based rock of the Rolling Stones, Aerosmith or early AC/DC. Lars was studying "looser" sounds than those such fastidious inspirations as Judas Priest or Iron Maiden.

Only two and a half years after *Justice* and it started to seem like a curious artifact—so much had their view of metal shifted. After the *Garage* EP, they wanted that rawness to rub off on their next album, but after six months of work, it lacked spontaneity. To Lars, the songs on *Justice* would later sound a bit sterile.

Slightly stronger is the reaction of Jason Newsted, who once remarked that he would rather quit Metallica and start an Elvis tribute band than record another album like . . . *And Justice for All.* As far as Jason was concerned, the bass was almost completely lost in the mix.

"*Justice* now sounds like it was recorded in a match-box. It was, 'Look at us, we can play all this intricate sideways stuff,' " Lars recalled, then added, "Well, so what? *Metallica* is more emotional. When it's angry it's more angry, when it's subtle it's more subtle. For the first time, we've done what was best for the big picture."

For the first time in their career, Metallica admitted that it would be okay if somebody else helped them look at that big picture. That man was Bob Rock.

Canadian album producer Bob Rock has achieved

fame as the man behind such top-selling albums as Bon Jovi's *Slippery When Wet,* Mötley Crüe's *Dr. Feelgood* and David Lee Roth's *A Little Ain't Enough.* In addition, Kirk was impressed with the way Rock had produced the Cult and Blue Murder. As James said of their new producer, "He opened our minds to a few things, that's all. There's no hurt in letting someone do their stuff, you can always say no."

For many in the metal community, the question was why did Metallica say yes? Skilled behind the big board as Rock may have been, he was widely considered too commercial a producer for a band that had so steadfastly eschewed the hollow victories of corporate rock. Would this start Metallica—who had so far made scarcely a false step in its career—down the slippery slope of radio-fodder commercialism?

Lars's reaction: "There's been this mass hysteria over nothing." Bob Rock wouldn't transform Metallica into Journey only with scarier fans, but he could be their passport out of what had been a creatively constricting place—the top of the thrash heap.

When a caller on an MTV interview show asked Kirk why Metallica chose Bob Rock to produce the album, he replied, "We liked the sound of his name." (And yes, it *is* his real name.)

When the band returned to One on One studios in late 1990 to begin recording *Metallica,* Bob Rock was ready to make changes. He told them that he'd seen them in Vancouver on their last tour and didn't think their recordings did their live performances—for lack of a better word— *justice.*

In an early meeting with Lars, Rock told him that one area he really wanted to develop was James's voice. Lars was immediately engaged, as he'd felt for a long time that James had had it in him—but needed a strong producer to get it out. Rock wanted *Metallica* to showcase a James Hetfield with a greatly enhanced range and sense of nuance.

"We've always done things in whatever direction our heads have taken us," Lars commented to *Faces Rocks,* "but our heads have never taken us in the direction of letting someone else into that inner circle to throw stuff at us when we were making records." Bob Rock was allowed, as few have ever been, to sit in on a Metallica rehearsal. Jason remembers that when Rock joined them, he freely made suggestions. At first James would scowl, but most of the time, Jason says, they found Rock's advice to be right on the money.

If one of the guys was playing something that sounded bad to Rock, he'd say so. Kirk recalled to *Spin* his reaction to a Rock criticism: " '*What the fuck would you do?* '" to which Rock would reply, " 'Well, you should play more bluesy, sustained notes.' I'm listening, and I'm shocked because . . . for once he was right," Kirk admitted.

As opposed to the engineer who let Metallica produce themselves, Flemming Rasmussen, Bob Rock was a willful presence who took on the sometimes unpleasant task of slightly shifting the direction of a philosophically entrenched rock'n'roll band. Knowing that what he proposed would often go against the Metallica grain, Rock would sometimes reassure the band that there would always be time to go back and rectify something of which they disapproved. In reality, there wasn't time, a fact well known to Bob Rock.

Bob Rock was dreadfully amused when he heard that Metallica never recorded live-in-the-studio. They had always recorded their parts separately. Not anymore. At the insistence of Bob Rock, all basic tracks for *Metallica* were recorded live, for spontaneity's sake. (And sometimes it would require over twenty takes to get the spontaneity right.) As Lars told *Music Express,* "We'd never really *had* anybody push us before."

Writing the material for *Metallica* took only two months. The band was actively applying the Reductive Method of Metallica again. They wanted to strip away the insanely relentless approach of *Justice* and declare themselves free from what they referred to as CNN-styled songs. They didn't want to continue to base their material on the issues they saw covered on the TV news. (To Metallica, CNN carried more weight than other news-gathering organizations—it's shown in hotel rooms all over the world.)

On a purely musical level, Lars believes that fear of inadequacy as players led the band into the expansive, tortuous riffing of *Puppets* and *Justice.* It was almost a way of showing off. "We were nineteen years old and thrown in at the deep end," Lars said in his own defense to *Rolling Stone.*

"James writes the best riffs in the world, and I think I've got a pretty good head for a song—what kinda feel it has, how the chorus should feel, what the bridges should be like," Lars said to *Music Express.* "But this time around we really wanted to keep it simple and keep it pounding."

For James, the streamlined vision was a return to the heart of metal. "To me, Metallica is still the guitar," he told the *Providence Journal-Bulletin.* "Songs like 'Through the Never' and 'Holier Than Thou' are more in-your-face than anything we've done."

When the band decided that simpler tunes were better, they didn't quite realize all the work that goes into a simple tune. As Lars commented to *Faces,* "All the great rock songs of the last 20 years, like 'Smoke on the Water' or 'Whole Lotta Love' are all one-riff songs."

* * *

Describing "Enter Sandman" to *Rolling Stone,* James said, "Here's the new vibe gone to the extreme." And extreme it is. A sharp depiction of a child's garden of nightmares, the unstoppable "Sandman" dream-riff comes in on spacy arpeggiated guitars, then turns massive, running through the song like an eight-lane superhighway. At one instant, a mildly threatening, Hetfieldian "Boo!" is tossed into the mix.

James's chilling recital of the child's bedtime prayer accents the introspective themes on *Metallica.* ("The God That Failed" also has a strong childhood theme.) James believed that his new perspective on childhood was tied in with his recent reacquaintance with his father.

Kirk told *Loud* that "Enter Sandman," the first single from *Metallica,* was "just an obvious choice for us and 'The Unforgiven' is our second single. It was just obvious. It was screaming out, 'Release me!' "

"Sad but True" is a point-of-view song sung by the demons inside us all. With another heavily cinematic intro, the monolithic, quavering, vaguely Arabic megariff of "Sad but True" stomps its way into the song, matched by a lost-soul choir of guitar sirens rising up into the mix. The stinging "Sad but True" riff was stumbled upon while the band was in the studio recording their cover of Queen's "Stone Cold Crazy."

An abstract depiction of the unbreakable human will, "The Unforgiven" takes James's snarling vocals and turns them on a melancholy chorus that's catchy and affecting.

"Wherever I May Roam" is an ode to personal freedom, with some reference to Metallica's unusually nomadic lifestyle, though in fact the song's title was pulled from a Tom Waits lyric. Thumb cymbals and James's sitar conjure up faraway places, and then another neo–Middle Eastern riff is jogged into a metallic one. James's emphasis was on the necessity of adapting yourself to all situations—the kind of outdoorsy, even survivalist thought James might get when he goes hunting.

On "Wherever I May Roam," "Of Wolf and Man" and a number of other songs on *Metallica,* the vocals are *singing* the song's hook, rather than being in counterpoint to the main, guitar-played hook. One principal achievement of *Metallica* is that at last Metallica's vocals were put on equal footing with the guitars.

A stern proclamation of peace-through-strength, "Don't Tread on Me" leads off with a musical quote of "I Want to Live in America" from Leonard Bernstein's *West Side Story.* As the song progresses, its escalating chords challenge—even threaten—like evenly matched armies before the clash.

If the song has any political significance, that significance would be about two centuries old. "Don't Tread on Me" was inspired by the Revolutionary War–era flag of Culpepper's Minutemen of Virginia. (A re-creation of the flag adorned the studio where *Metallica* was recorded.) The snake and slogan "Don't Tread on Me" were a common part of eighteenth-century political symbology.

"On *Justice* we stayed to the shitty side—not 'America sucks' but pointing out the scary parts," James explained to *Spin.* "But certain people, they're way out of hand with that shit. Go fucking somewhere else then, man." Metallica has always mirrored their audience, which includes its strong conservative streak.

Most critics decried as jingoistic the inclusion of "Don't Tread on Me," and considered the coiled-snake flag on the cover as part of some post–Gulf War victory dance. In fact, the song was written before war with Iraq was by any means certain. Nonetheless, Hetfield admits that there is a certain proud nationalism to the song—partially as a counterweight to all his criticism of the government in . . . *And Justice for All.*

"That tune had been around a long time before any-body even knew who Saddam Hussein was," Kirk explained to *Thrasher.* "A lot of people misinterpreted that as being a pro-war song like, 'Let's go out there and kick ass.' That song is basically about the 'Don't Tread on Me' flag that was used in the Revolutionary War. It was a huge misunder-standing based on a very wrong assumption. People are quick to assume things. I'm not for war in any shape or form; I'm pretty much a chicken shit."

A call to earthly elementalism, "Of Wolf and Man" takes an extreme back-to-nature position that suggests the wolf inside the man manifests itself more than just psychologically. With a philosophy not too different from that of *The Howling,* "Of Wolf and Man" is driven by a sharp, canine-toothed riff, with James's vocals shape shifting a bit themselves.

"The Struggle Within" returns to a stops-out negativity

The multiple Grammy winners smile for the camera in 1992. *Courtesy John Mantel-Sipa.*

that approaches "Harvester of Sorrow" in its relentlessness. Composed out of different segments, tempo shifts and synchronized guitars, this song would appeal to diehard *Justice* fans. (On which album it would have to be about twice as long.)

The most unexpected song on *Metallica* is "Nothing Else Matters." More than a love song, "Nothing Else Matters" is an open-hearted, soul-bearing expression of devotion. Throughout its gorgeous yet simple verse and chorus, gentle acoustic guitars shimmer in the mix, complemented by a forty-piece orchestra. New Age/soundtracks success story Michael Kamen led the orchestra, which was bound to cause alarm among the old-line fans. Then again, anyone who thinks an orchestra is saccharine doesn't realize where the concept of the power chord originated.

With "Nothing Else Matters" the band sought to start a song off gently, like "Fade to Black" or "One," and only maintain the song's steady power—not to let it go ballistic as the others do. James was working on the song in a Canadian hotel room. ("I wrote it when I was lonely on the road," he told the *Providence Journal-Bulletin.*) When Lars heard the song later, he was much more impressed than surprised. Or as James told Rolling Stone, "The word *harmonies* has never been a bad word in the Metallica camp."

As has become Metallica tradition, these recording sessions have also yielded another pair of obscure cover tunes. "Killing Time," originally recorded by Sweet Savage in 1981, contains some sharp, rockin' riffing and a snappy call-and-response chorus. This is a Metallica cover that goes all the way back to the beginning.

Sweet Savage was an Irish NWOBHM band whose fortunes turned around when they supported Motörhead on the latter's Irish tour in the early eighties. "Killing Time" was the B side of the Irish group's first single, "Take No

Prisoners." Sweet Savage guitarist Vivian Campbell later went on to fill the late Steve Clark's guitar spot in superstar pop-metal band Def Leppard.

The second cover was "So What?," first by grunge-punks the Anti-Nowhere League. A roaring, engine-gunning power-riff punches up a song so wholeheartedly filthy and generously perverse that it was destined to make the PMRC filing cabinets flip over in disbelief. Naturally, it's so extreme that no one could possibly take it seriously—except for literal-minded anti-rock crusaders.

A play on the British Anti-Nazi League, the Anti-Nowhere League was an intentionally disreputable punk-rock burlesque act that recorded songs like "I Hate ... People" and "Let's Break the Law." The Metallica version of "So What?" was released as an extra track on Japanese pressings of *Metallica*.

Ever since "Hit the Lights," Metallica's music has owed a debt to movie soundtracks. Darkly cinematic riffs run through Metallica's music like a madness-inducing blood-line. The work of spaghetti-western-soundtrack composer Ennio Morricone was always influential, as his music was practically a rite of commencement before their concerts. James and Jason are especially fond of Morricone—his soundtrack albums can be found all over the studios in which Metallica has recorded. And somewhere, teased the band, *somewhere* in the mix of *Metallica* lurks a sample of some piece of Morricone music.

When *Metallica* hit the stores, fans were greeted by a nearly black cover bearing only the faintest outlines of Metallica's omnipresent vampire-fanged logo. "It's just a desire to get away from all that metal bullshit, all the cartoon imagery and all the other crap," Lars explained. "Bands have all these silly mascots. A lot of people are going to be whining about it, but where our state of mind is at, it's just *right.*" It was as if Metallica was trying to let the old Metallica fade away with this new release. The plain album sleeve was a way of escaping the images the band felt it had to conjure up for the public. Also, by giving the listener nothing to look at, Metallica tried to keep the focus on the songs. "We were even talking about not calling the album anything. It's basically called *Metallica* by default," Lars told *Rolling Stone.* Immediately, rock critics everywhere started drawing the obvious parallels between the all-black Metallica album called simply *Metallica* and the all-white Beatles album called simply *The Beatles.* If there were any comparisons to be made, the critics didn't get too much farther than that.

After two months of songwriting and ten months of studio time, *Metallica* would ultimately cost in the neighborhood of a million dollars to produce. Band, label execs and management thought it deserved a launch that nobody would ever forget.

Elektra VP of marketing David Bither dreamed up the idea of a large-scale, free-admission listening party for fans, held at some oversized venue. After plans fell through to hold more than one listening party, Madison Square Garden was the chosen place.

Tickets for the August 3, 1991, event were given away at New York–area record retailers Nobody Beats the Wiz. On July 20, the first day of distribution, sixteen thousand of the twenty-one thousand tickets had been snapped up by fans. Tickets were supposed to be issued only two to a customer, but even only vaguely resourceful fans found it easy to walk out with as many as eight tickets at a time. Tickets weren't even collected at the Garden.

Despite the high number of distributed tickets, the number of fans in attendance was put at nine thousand fans according to *Billboard,* although an Elektra ad in that same magazine started the number as fourteen thousand. The entire album was played, along with video interviews and other footage of the band. When the last song ended, the Metallicans came out and thanked everyone for coming. They also took that opportunity to work the crowd into a rowdy twenty-eighth birthday greeting to James.

At the listening party, Z-Rock's Mad Max Hammer hosted the *Metallica* world radio premiere. Although record labels are often more than happy to let a brand-new artist's album be played over the radio in its entirety, it's a lot less likely to happen with an established act like Metallica.

"We just decided to have a listening party for a few close friends—it got a little bit bigger than we thought it would turn out," Kirk told MTV. "It was a lot of fun. It worked out really well. . . . I was out and amongst the fans. The lights were down and I saw this guy sitting in a wheelchair and I tapped him on the shoulder and he looked up at me and he kinda jumped. And I said, 'How do you like the album?' And he goes, 'Oh, it's great!' And then I walked off and I looked behind me and he was, like, following me. And then it got bigger and so I had to get out of there."

Although Lars wasn't being followed around like some *Life of Brian*–styled reluctant savior, he also found the experience peculiar. As he remarked to MTV, "It was weird just walking around the corridors of Madison Square Garden and your album's playing up there and there's ten thousand people sitting up there and it was really uncomfortable. I was more nervous that day than I've ever been for anything else with Metallica."

The Metallica fans surely approved. So confident of *Metallica*-mania were some stores in the huge Camelot Music chain that they opened their doors at 12:01 A.M. in order to let fans buy the album the minute it was officially released.

19

> "For our album *Master of Puppets* we were going to have a video that featured Howdy Doody with a syringe, but we didn't do that, either."
>
> —Kirk Hammett, on Metallica's previous rock video ideas (*San Jose Mercury News*)

In the wake of the surprisingly successful "One" videoclip, Metallica reunited with director Michael Salomon to document the American section of the Damaged Justice tour. Shot over three nights in the northwestern cities of Portland, Seattle and Spokane, this video record was to be as authentic as possible. "If a string breaks or I break a drumstick, we'll show it," Lars told *Metal Edge*.

Realism is paramount to Lars, who also told the same publication, "So much of a Metallica gig is being there and feeling the kick drum in your stomach. We want to make sure that can be transferred to a TV screen."

Michael Salomon used around a half dozen cameras to shoot the sensitive story of Metallica and Doris, their amazing exploding girlfriend. Several years after the footage was shot, it remains "in the can."

If this footage ever does see the light of day, it may contain further evidence of Metallica lip-synching. After taping part of a Metallica performance, Michael Salomon asked the band if they'd do that part just once more for the cameras. "They weren't crazy about it," Salomon recalls, "and when I shot the stage show, I had them play back a couple of things because they had some effects that were happening on the stage with the statue exploding and all that. And I wasn't a hundred percent sure that I captured it the way I needed to get it on video, so I had them go back and play it. They were very reluctant to do it at first, but after they got used to it, they were actually getting into it. . . . I don't think they realized how many times you have to do it over and over again, and I think they were a little frustrated at that. But they were good sports about it."

"To us, video was always like this sort of corporate thing that had something to do with business and marketing— all that kind of stuff," Lars once told *Rip* magazine. To change this view and to start releasing music videos like any other rock'n'roll band was not an easy turnabout for Metallica. Annoying music videos seemed to be coming out of the woodwork. When *Spin* asked rock stars about their least favorite examples, Lars responded: "R.E.M.'s 'Shiny Happy People' video! I have never wanted to do a John Bonham with my television, but this is the closest it's ever come!" Lars refers of course to the late Led Zeppelin drummer, whose approval of television shows was expressed in far more visceral ways than Nielsen points.

"The video format is very different now than what we were used to in the early and mid-eighties," Kirk told *The Island Ear*. "All the videos that were being made back then were just plain stupid as far as metal bands were concerned; bands always performing onstage or bimbos running around—and that kinda turned us off to it. We've opened up our minds and our perspectives a bit more now and we've found that we can experiment with the video-format and be creative with it."

Enter Sandman, the first clip from *Metallica*, stands as the band's most effective video ever. *Sandman* was directed by longtime music video ace Wayne Isham, the man responsible for many videos by Def Leppard, Bon Jovi and a host of others.

The cruel landscape of *Enter Sandman* is a child's nightmare. With the visuals slightly, dreamily blurred, we see an all-American, Norman Rockwell–ish boy's room—and a kid who dreams he's stuck floundering underwater. In another instant, he'll take a terrifying fall from a rooftop directly into . . . his own bed. It seems no longer to be such a safe place.

As narrators of the video, Metallica is shown in a succession of still-looking shots. Piling up on top of each other like a grisly series of police photos dropped onto a desktop, the band is seen through a sort of crude animation. Cleverly dodging lip-synching, the group appears only this way throughout the video.

Nightmare imagery abounds. A snake slithers over the child in his bed, but worse, his omnipresent what's-under-the-bed impulse is horribly rewarded. The floor is crawling with snakes. Cannily, the video follows dream logic and all of a sudden the child's bed is out in a bright open field. Making the Hitchcockian point that the safest-looking places are really the most dangerous, an unstoppable eighteen-wheel tractor-trailer truck bears down on the bed like the maniacal Macks from Stephen King's *Maximum Overdrive*. The child tries to escape, and the truck splinters his bed in perfect synch with Hetfield's evil-natured "Boo!" The kid manages to jump out of the way, but skids over a cliff—and into another long spiraling fall into bed. *Enter Sandman* concludes with slow strobes across the wrinkled forehead of an old man—who could quite easily be the same person as the dreaming boy.

When the ideas were being considered for this video, James suggested that they depict a mother's worst nightmare. Her baby sits in its crib with snakes crawling all over it, and the mother can't get to the child. James thought that it would be possible to use a real infant in the same crib as the real snakes. The video people blanched at the idea, and it was thankfully scrapped.

Directed by Matt Mahurin, *The Unforgiven* is another video that—according to Kirk anyway—closely follows the song's lyrics. These claims *should* be verifiable, yet *The Unforgiven* has been judged by fans to be the most impenetrable representation of a Metallica song ever committed to video.

Shot entirely in black and white, *The Unforgiven* opens on odd textures: a sharply sculpted surface of mud and puddles, with a small child playing in one of them. Soon, a cabal of three mysterious men embrace. With no particular niches in reality for the viewer to get a grip on, these images are obscure.

Shots of the band seem to show them in a soft-focus otherworld, apart from the confusing drama being played out in the rest of the video.

The little boy is confined to some sort of dank place—a sewer or aqueduct. In a more literal expansion of the old man–young man impressions of *Sandman,* the viewer is led to believe that the boy is aging throughout—from childhood to middle age to old age. (Although it was beginning to look like Metallica was starting some sort of wizened old man cult, the picture of the old man dancing during the guitar solo is hard to forget.)

Images of time passing, blood being drawn, an escape hatch gradually cut into a wall, and a key all figure into the video's themes of an endless struggle for freedom. The video's final image of an old man sleeping in the spot of sunlight on the concrete floor is a disturbing and seemingly unresolved picture.

Mahurin also created a special cut of *The Unforgiven,* which ran over ten minutes long. The same images as the regular version appear in the extended cut, although there are no shots of the band and no music for a substantial portion of the clip. MTV made a special premiere of the extended *Unforgiven* clip, but aired it only once.

"Nothing Else Matters," the third single, was portrayed by candid footage of the band in the studio while they recorded the song. If viewers think that it was lucky of the video crew to catch James just as he sang the song's basic vocal track, they'd better think again. The footage used in *Nothing Else Matters* was drawn from something called *The Metallica Sessions 1990–1991.*

In these sessions, the band was taped cutting all those basic tracks that Bob Rock insisted they record together. So, whatever particular take of the "Nothing" vocals was finally used on the album, there would be corresponding footage of the actual performance available. This is yet another way to get out of lip-synching. If James or anyone in the band needed to be shown singing or playing, there's no need to simulate it: the original event can be used.

Nothing Else Matters depicts studio life over the course of one song, and has no particular relationship to the song's lyrical content.

The video opens with scenes of an empty One on One studio—complete with unused drum kit, Culpepper's Revolutionary War flag, Marshall amps and Metallica-stenciled flight cases.

In a few moments, the studio comes to life with band members and studio crew. Jason, correctly anticipating fans' in-concert reaction to the song, demonstratively waves a match up in the air during its playback. Kirk wears a shirt advertising Lovecraft-derived movie *The Re-Animator*. The video further details Jason as he plays pool, Kirk as he flings ice cream at the camera, and a poster of hunky rocker Kip Winger that seems to have had darts thrown at it. With Metallica's removal of their instruments, the song ends.

The fourth Metallica video, *Wherever I May Roam,* creates a similar effect, only in a concert environment. This video, however, does adhere somewhat to the song's lyrics— since the themes of mobility are well expressed by this mini-movie of a band on the road.

Shot by the video crew that accompanied Metallica throughout their 1991–92 tour, *Wherever I May Roam* offers documentary evidence of what went into keeping that tour on the road. The band plays for soundcheck in front of an eerily empty arena. Yet as the camera dollies around James Hetfield, the empty hall suddenly becomes a sold-out hall, filled with thousands of fist-pumping Metallicatz. Not a strict concert document, this video also shows James playing the guitar solo in a sweaty T-shirt and Kirk visiting a musical instrument shop to goof around with an electric mandolin. And in a classic Metallica moment, Kirk obligingly autographs the shaved part of a fan's mohawked head. Rolling tourbuses and other signs of rock transiency conclude the *Wherever I May Roam* video.

* * *

And there will be more Metallica road footage to come. On the 1991–92 tour, Wayne Isham filmed Metallica over two nights in San Diego. There is some thought to matching up the Isham material with some taken by Michael Salomon in Seattle during the Justice tour. For the time being, however, the footage stays in an ever-more-crowded "can."

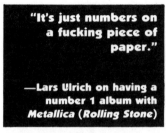

20

By the nineties, Metallica was doing more than just attracting attention in the music business: they were the heavy metal toast of the music business. Which means that music business executives who'd never heard of Megadeth, Slayer or Anthrax would say, "Oh, Metallica. I've heard of them." The music industry was clearly taking notice of Metallica. (And if Metallica was smart, it would be sure to take no notice of the music business.)

"It's interesting. If you think back a couple of years ago, people would never, ever give a band like Metallica a chance," Lars Ulrich told journalist Harold DeMuir. "It was like, 'Yeah, Metallica, sure,' I think there's a lot of people in record companies who are unaware of what's going on on the street. It's very difficult to sit up here on the twenty-first floor and really feel what's happening all the way down on the gutter level."

Metallica weren't in the gutter when Michael Alago of Elektra Records found them, but his instincts did bode well for the metal scene. With any luck, bands that were designated as "underground" simply because they didn't have that many fans would be given a shot topside. "We've always had our own way of doing things, and Elektra and our management have been very open-minded about letting us do our own thing," Lars continued to DeMuir. "We've proven to them that it can be done. Everything we've done has always been on our own terms—I know, you read these magazines and every band says, 'We never compromise,' but in our case, it's true."

Record and management companies do have *strategies,* however, and the best companies tailor their strategies to their artists' musical personalities. Even though rock videos were always considered inimical to the Metallica ethic, the videos were made to conform to that ethic. Through MTV, the Metallica audience expanded. James now notices older fans at the gigs, possibly metal fans of the seventies whose first new album in years was *Metallica.*

Radio listeners, long ignorant of a widely unprogrammed Metallica, were in the late eighties starting to get the message. Originally, new metal was accorded a time slot here or there on alternative-dominated radio stations—some, like Seton Hall University's WSOU, were more fully committed. All-metal commercial radio stations were few and far between, but included KNAC in Long Beach, California, and Z-Rock on the Dallas-based Satellite Radio Network. Other syndicated shows, such as *Metal Shop,* preferred trad-metal styles like Van Halen's.

When program director Lee Abrams arrived at Z-Rock, he found the station's playlist to be "scattered." A Slayer track would be followed by Elvis Presley, or other such odd combinations. Abrams hired deejays who loved the new metal and infused the station with a loony, over-the-edge style. Abrams made the programming more metal-intensive and started broadcasting live concerts—such as Metallica and Queensrÿche.

"When I got here around '89, 'Breadfan' was ridiculously popular," Abrams recalls. "Every time you played it the phones would explode and we started playing it more and it just snowballed." The conventional wisdom that kept Metallica off the radio—that they just weren't "big" enough—was turning out to be nonsense. Aside from playing the new Metallica singles as they were released, Z-Rock went "deep catalog" and played older songs that the fans still loved. " 'Fade to Black' is an anthem," Abrams notes, and adds, "[With] Metallica, and bands of that stature, we tend to go real deep. Play pretty much anything. We also have a thing called *The Mighty Met*, which is an hour of Metallica every ten-thirty on Saturday nights. We saw that Metallica fans were so loyal, we decided, 'Let's give these guys their own show.' It was sort of experimental at first, then it got so big."

Selling a loud, rowdy and generally unkempt genre like metal to often-stuffy broadcasters reminded Lee Abrams of the earliest days of album-oriented rock (AOR) stations, when hippies were still a perceived threat. These station owners weren't interested in their airwaves being used by the "flag-burning, drug-addict hippies that listen to that." When Abrams proposed a syndicated all-metal format, some reacted by saying, according to Abrams, " 'Yeah, we know that these bands are big, but it's all devil-worshiping punks who listen to it and we're not putting that on our station.' Following the same pattern as AOR, just a few success stories and people realize that it's not so bad. It's pretty normal. But it *did* face the same problems early AOR faced."

Indeed, metal radio isn't the only thing that sold big with the name Metallica attached to it. Vast numbers of guitar-, bass- or drum-playing fans buy Metallica's sheet music every year. Cherry Lane Music, Metallica's sheet-music publisher, sells easy and not-so-easy books with music to all the songs for a given Metallica album. The company also publishes a series, *Heavy Metal Guitar Songbooks*, that includes songs from *Kill 'Em All* through *Metallica*. Cherry Lane routinely reports Metallica sheet music sales as number 1 amongst its best-selling folios.

Although James Hetfield can't read music, kids will approach him with their Metallica songbooks for him to autograph. If some young musician tells James that he finds some passage particularly difficult, James will quite seriously point to some chord or measure, tell the kid it's *wrong* and then make some meaningless, random "correction" in the book.

When *Kill 'Em All* was initially released on Megaforce in 1983, it never made a dent in the music charts. It *did* enter the charts with its Elektra re-release in 1986. Its long stand on the album charts peaked in February of 1988 at number 120.

Ride the Lightning entered the chart in the fall of '84 and rose to number 100 by the following spring. The album would remain on the chart for just shy of a year. *Ride the Lightning* was certified gold by the Recording Industry Association of America (RIAA), for sales of 500,000 units. In 1992, *Ride the Lightning* reached double-platinum in sales, with over two million copies sold.

Entering the charts only a week before the re-released *Kill 'Em All* in the spring of '86, *Master of Puppets* rose to number 29—Metallica's first Top 40 chart success. *Puppets* would stay on the chart for seventy-two weeks. It ultimately went platinum, and also created a coattail effect, renewing enough interest in the entire Metallica catalog to bring *Kill 'Em All* and *Ride the Lightning* back onto the chart.

Metallica's cheapest new release, *The $5.98 EP: Garage Days Rerevisited,* entered the album chart in September of

'87, and one month later went *Puppets* one better by hitting number 28. Its chart residency lasted thirty weeks.

In chartland, the jackpot was finally hit with ... *And Justice for All*. Entering the chart in September of 1988 at number 35, it only took four weeks for the album to bullet its way to number 6 on the *Billboard* Top Pop Albums chart. It stayed on the chart for eighty-three weeks.

Manager Cliff Burnstein tried not to overplay the success story of *Justice,* observing fairly that the album's popularity was right in line with the platinum certification of *Puppets* and the gold certifications for *Lightning* and *Garage Days.* (Even the *Cliff 'Em All* home video had gone platinum.) Burnstein did note that they sold the same number of copies of *Puppets* in three years as they sold of *Justice* in two weeks.

Metallica received their third Grammy nomination for best metal performance, vocal or instrumental, for their cover of Queen's "Stone Cold Crazy," which was recorded for the Elektra Records anniversary album *Rubaiyat.* Their competition in the category was Suicidal Tendencies' *Lights ... Camera ... Revolution,* Judas Priest's *Painkiller,* Anthrax's *Persistence of Time* and Megadeth's *Rust in Peace.* (Amusing that the 1991 Grammy Awards would honor so many people who used to hang around the Yonkers Music Building in 1983.) Metallica won the category and collected their second Grammy.

The band didn't show up at the awards show, because, according to Lars, they had little enthusiasm for a nominating group that chose a song recorded in about a quarter of an hour. Still, for a quick job, Metallica did it right. The old Queen riff for "Stone Cold Crazy" holds up very well for the nineties, and the song's stop-start pacing is just right for mosh-inspiring Metallica.

The Frayed Ends of Metal

If ... *And Justice for All* hit the sales jackpot for the band, then *Metallica* broke the bank. In its first week of release, it shipped 2.2 million copies, bumping Natalie Cole's *Unforgettable* album out of the number 1 position. Record chain Nobody Beats the Wiz reported that the album was responsible for its biggest single day of album sales in ten years. Elektra initially ordered a pressing of 1.4 million copies, but within four days added 800,000 albums to the order.

During that first week, *Metallica* sold an estimated 600,000 copies. The country's biggest record retailer, Musicland Stores Corporation, said that the album sold just under 100,000 copies in its stores alone. Camelot Music estimated *its* sales to be between 80,000 and 90,000. An executive at Wherehouse Entertainment said that *Metallica* sold as many albums in one day as Van Halen's *For Unlawful Carnal Knowledge* sold in one week. In its first year, *Metallica* would go "quadruple-platinum," or sell over five million albums, and would remain in the Top 40 for the better part of a year.

Record-industry successes fly by thick and fast, but to reach the number 1 spot on the *Billboard* chart immediately puts a rock group in the company of the angels. And as soon as it got into the stores, *Metallica* had a reserved spot on cloud nine. Overseas, the story was roughly the same. *Metallica* went to number 1 on album charts in England, Germany, Switzerland, Canada, Australia, New Zealand and Norway.

Lars, James, Kirk and Jason were in Budapest, Hungary, on tour with AC/DC for their second Monsters of Rock jaunt when the fax came in from the home office in New York that *Metallica* had just gone to number 1. Sitting in his Hungarian hotel room, Lars studied the fax and realized that he just couldn't get ecstatic over it. If there was some sort

James rocks Wembley at the Freddie Mercury
tribute concert. *Courtesy Andrew Murray-Sipa.*

of transformation that was supposed to take place when you became a number 1–selling artist, Lars wasn't feeling it. Jason had never given the idea of going to number 1 a thought, assuming that their genre would be a permanent handicap.

In chartland, 1991 was metal's biggest year. Pop or urban styles customarily top the charts, but in the summer of '91, metal got its revenge. Hard-rockers Skid Row entered the chart at number 1, as did Van Halen. After *Metallica* claimed the top spot, Guns n' Roses' two simultaneously released albums crowded around number 1. Cynical, curmudgeonly Lars wasn't having any of it, though—he saw the 1991 metal chart assault as having more to do with plain old lucky timing than anything else.

But the primacy on the *Billboard* charts during the summer of '91 had much to do with a change in the way music charts were compiled. Traditionally, *Billboard* charts were assembled from phoned-in sales reports from individual retailers, who would give the rankings in sales from number 1 onwards. In 1991, *Billboard* began using data from SoundScan, a system which immediately registered the sale of a record by its scanned bar code. Under SoundScan, chart information was available faster and with greater accuracy—and it also gave good representation to those large chains with scanning cash registers. SoundScan would allow the charts to recognize the hitherto-unseen metal majority.

Metal bands were also starting to make megadeals in the wake of the summer of '91. Elektra signed Mötley Crüe to a deal worth more than $35 million, and Aerosmith's deal with Columbia Records was said to be worth $30 million.

Programmer Lee Abrams sees the metal trend as lasting the lifetimes of its listeners. "The music that people like between about sixteen and twenty years of age tends to be what they like for life," he explains. "There's a lot of people just getting into metal when they're sixteen/twenty years old, the musically formative years. And the myth is, they'll turn twenty-four/twenty-five and start liking Neil Diamond. It just doesn't happen. They just grow up with this music ... I can see fathers in the year 2020 going to their kids and saying, 'How can you listen to this garbage that's out now? You should be listening to stuff your mom and I grew up with, like Metallica.' "

In February of 1992, Metallica appeared on yet another Grammy broadcast and was again nominated. Their competition for best metal performance with vocal was Anthrax for *Attack of the Killer B's*; Soundgarten for *Badmotorfinger*; Motörhead for *1916*; and Megadeth (misspelled "Megadeath" on the TV chyron) for *Hangar 18*.

But before the award was given, Metallica performed "Enter Sandman" on the vast Radio City Music Hall stage. The shirtless Lars was featured prominently, flailing away behind his double Tama bass drums. The camera rode on a roaming, Peter Pan's–eye view of the set to zero in on James's glowering face as he performed the vocals. Giant, multiscreen monitors flanked the band, showing the "Enter Sandman" video. (The day before the broadcast, during Metallica's soundcheck, Lars was increasingly frustrated by the Grammy producers' insistence that the band somehow play *in synch* with the video. Realizing the annoying difficulty in this, Lars stood up on his drum stool to voice his displeasure. When the show aired, there was no attempt for the band to follow along with the video.

After the "Enter Sandman" performance, presenters Robbie Robertson and Little Steven Van Zandt announced that *Metallica* was the winner. James Hetfield grimaced at

the backstage camera as the band walked out to the po-
dium, Lars still gripping an Evian bottle in hand.

"Ho, ho, ho, ho!" Lars began as he wiped himself off
with a towel. "Couldn't you give us a few more minutes
after that? Anyway, let's get on with it." In a clownish gesture, Jason helped mop Lars's forehead. Lars unhesitatingly
responded, "Thank you. You want a job?"

An acceptance speech is a dangerous opportunity for
a garrulous soul like Lars Ulrich. He began, "Let's see, I think
the first thing we gotta do is . . . we gotta thank Jethro Tull
for not putting out an album this year, right?" Lars laughed
savagely at his revenge for Tull's inconceivable victory over
. . . And Justice for All.

"I wanna thank—this is very important," Lars continued, "I wanna thank all the radio stations and MTV. Without
whom, without whom . . . *all this was possible anyway.*
Whoa! . . . Just kidding, guys, just kidding . . . wanna thank
all the stations for coming around finally and understanding
what the hell Metallica was all about. And then, obviously,
which is the most important," as Lars was being motioned
from off-camera to wrap it up, "*yeah, I know, get on with
it, right*—is that I wanna thank all the thousands or millions
of Metallica fans out there who've been following us for
ten/eleven years now and and who've made all this possible
and proving to everybody out there in the industry and so
on that if you stick to your guts and just do what you want
to do that all this will happen sooner or later and people
will wake up, you know what I mean? So thanks a lot."
Holding their awards aloft in thanks, Metallica walked off.

"We're the token metal act on these award shows,"
Jason told the *New York Post.* And James added, to the
same publication, "Less jaws drop now, but I still see some,
and I like that." Of course, the band's new widespread
popularity from *Metallica* has had its pitfalls. Mainstream

interviewers, just barely aware of this latest album, often ask the band when they plan to start work on their second record.

The Grammy awards are not the only official recognition that Metallica had received. Their hometown music awards—the Bay Area Music Awards, otherwise known as the Bammies—have shown their appreciation for Metallica as well. In 1991, Metallica won a total of four Bammies: for outstanding album, outstanding metal album, outstanding song ("Enter Sandman") and outstanding drummer/percussionist (Lars).

When the music-industry trade magazine *HITS* launched a new section devoted to metal, Lars, James, Kirk and Jason appeared in the front of the issue, gleefully mooning the camera. Was this symbolic of their overall relationship to the music biz?

"We always wanted to be different from the rest of the music business," Lars told *People*. "It's too classic: You make a record, you make a video. We were the first to give the finger to the music industry in America." Of course, this is not particularly true—plenty of musicians have given the finger to the music industry. But Metallica is one of the few bands in a strong enough position for the music industry to not give them the finger right back.

Perhaps Metallica's relationship to the music biz can be encapsulated in this statement Lars made to Harold DeMuir: "From the time we started, back in the garage in L.A. in 1981, it's always been about having fun. I still look at us as four drinking buddies united around the music. It's cool if we've opened some doors that weren't opened before and it's cool if we've made people realize that there is a market for bands like this. But that's not what it's about— it's just about us having fun playing our music."

21

When Metallica signed on to the 1991 Monsters of Rock tour, they were glad to return to the mania, the interaction, the camaraderie and the downright *béorscipe* of festival touring. This second Monsters outing was headlined by AC/DC, with Mötley Crüe, Queensrÿche and the Black Crowes.

Lars was miffed at the prospect that all the bands on this Monsters tour were reformed drinkers. "Maybe the Crowes drink," Lars said, and then added in reference to their rail-like vocalist Chris Robinson, "or we could at least fatten that singer up."

The greatest satisfaction for Metallica in the Monsters tour was the chance to play with AC/DC. Seeing Angus Young strike those thunder-from-down-under powerchords with Brian Johnson wailing like a big, aggravated insect—this was metal abandon at its most primal. By Lars's count, AC/DC were the last metal legends for Metallica to play with, joining a list that includes Deep Purple, Ozzy Osbourne, Van Halen, Aerosmith, Motörhead and Iron Maiden.

The MOR tour took the metal mavens throughout Europe, to such venues as the oft-played Castle Donington and the Hippodrome de Vincennes racetrack outside of Paris. Most significant for Lars was Metallica's concert in his birthplace of Copenhagen. Their venue was the Gentofte Stadium—Lars's "home team" field when he was a little boy. He'd played there as a kid, and now played there as an adult.

Metallica's MOR set was seventy-five minutes in length: not great, but certainly enough to delight the old-timers with a churnin' chesnut like "Whiplash," or to set the stadiums afire with Bic flames at the opening chords of "One." And the Metallifans could check out Jason's wavy mane dripping with sweat as he joined James on vocals for the "Master of Puppets–Seek and Destroy" medley or Lars pounding his skins bare on encore rocker "Battery."

Of all the songs from *Metallica,* the only two played at the MOR were "Enter Sandman" and "Sad but True." Metallica's tried-and-true crowd-pleasing festival philosophy still makes room for as many old favorites as possible.

"It's cool. You get to play to like forty thousand or sixty thousand people every night," Lars recalled, with the caveat, "That's the cool part. The uncool part is that you have a lot of days off, and when you're sitting in southern Germany, in Oldenburg, that's when the Monsters of Rock tour is not so cool and what we do is think of being in America."

If there was a time on the MOR tour that Lars thought about America *least,* it would've been during Metallica's stop in the former Soviet Union. A special September 28 concert had been arranged at the little-used Tushino Airfield outside of Moscow. In many respects, the concert was the still-crumbling government's official thank-you to the nation's young people for their part in defeating the attempted coup the month before. The only other time this many metal bands played on Soviet soil was in 1989, when Lenin Stadium hosted Ozzy Osbourne, Bon Jovi and Mötley Crüe for a charity benefit.

Metallica and Co. arrived in Moscow the night before the gig. After arriving at their hotel to drop off their things and toss back a few beers, James, Lars and members of the Metallica crew hopped into a couple of cabs and headed back into the Moscow night.

At two A.M. they watched the changing of the guard at Lenin's tomb. After that, they drove to the Russian Federation Building (also known as the Russian White House), where a month earlier Boris Yeltsin grabbed the world's attention by standing atop a tank to defy the coup.

There the Metallicans met the young Russians living in a tent city on the square as an ongoing memorial and protest. The Russians walked Lars, James and the others to the sites of barricades and to where three young Soviets were killed during the attempted coup by an unhinged soldier.

Some of the kids brought out guitars and sang a Scorpions song for the gathered Americans. The band felt awe over the power of music to give these young fans strength. To Lars, their love of the music was like Americans', but on a far more dramatic level.

When Lars walked into his hotel lobby, one fan had been waiting there for him. Instead of speaking, the fan just broke down crying. He found it nearly impossible to express how deeply touched he was that Metallica would actually come to Moscow to perform. For Lars and the others, the Russian trip had become a moving experience.

When discussing the Tushino show with *Rolling Stone*, Lars characterized a rock star's life as "going into a hotel and complaining that your room isn't as big as the next guy's." But in light of his Russian experiences, he added,

"You put it next to this and you realize it's about life and death."

The following day at Tushino, Metallica and the other Monsters played before an audience whose estimated size ranged from 150,000 to 500,000. The day-long, free-admission concert was produced by the Time Warner media conglomerate (which later released a home video of the concert, *For Those About to Rock*).

In traditional Soviet style, concert security was tight, rigid and threatening. Some arrests for drunkenness and rowdiness were reported. There were also counteraccusations of brutality by the police.

It was no slight to Metallica that of all the MOR bands, the Russians preferred AC/DC. Over the years, the Australian headbanging heroes have achieved cult status among the Russians—which should more than prove that the Russians are no different from the rest of the world.

22

In a gesture that must've evoked feelings of déjà vu for 1988, Metallica immediately followed the Monsters of Rock tour with an extensive international road trip to support *Metallica*.

The Wherever I May Roam arena tour ran from their October 12, 1991, show at the Peoria, Illinois, Civic Center well into the summer of 1992. Original plans were for Skid Row to open on the tour, but they declined. When Sebastian Bach and Co. had opened up for Bon Jovi on an '88 tour, it gave a huge boost to their popularity, but they insisted that their warm-up days were behind them.

During the planning of the Wherever I May Roam tour, some serious questions were raised. Could they sell enough tickets with the country mired in recession? This tour was estimated to cost a quarter of a million dollars a week to keep on the road. As soon as the money starts to dry up, the machinery grinds to a stop. Lars remembered hearing about the metal tours that lost out against the 1988 Monsters of Rock. "First the equipment goes home and then you go home," he told *Musician*.

On Wherever I May Roam, some venues presented Metallica with plaques to mark record attendance figures.

To keep Metallica on tour, it took a crew of about sixty people, from roadies to administrators. The band flew in a Gulfstream 1 private plane, decorated with the coiled-snake logo from *Metallica*. The airplane's gangway also had the band's name written on it.

The Wherever I May Roam caravan had a portable washer-dryer that took care of everybody's clothes while the band was playing. After each show, it took the crew about three hours to load up their twelve eighteen-wheel tractor-trailer trucks and get rolling.

There were well over a hundred dates on Wherever I May Roam. Over the course of the tour, Metallica would play concerts at Maple Leaf Gardens in Toronto, the Meadowlands in New Jersey, the Cow Palace in San Francisco and dozens of arenas in between. And Metallica was bringing something to these venues that they'd never seen before: SNAKES!

Well, not exactly snakes, but Metallica did come equipped with its own Snake Pit.

The band was in Amsterdam, when, on a layover between flights, someone drew a diamond shape on a paper napkin. Our next stage, he said, should look like this. The band liked this very sketchy idea for a new-concept stage. Their next idea was to have two drum kits—one on each side of the diamond. Then, Q Prime manager Peter Mensch came up with the idea of letting fans stand in the middle of the diamond—right smack in the center of the stage. To a Metallicat, they reasoned, it would be like sitting at the best table of a fine restaurant. Only much, much louder.

"It's pretty different from what anybody's ever seen

before," Lars said of the stage to MTV. "It's not theatrical. It's pretty clean."

Indeed, the new stage setup had no backdrops, no artwork, no enormous props. And yet the entire stage itself was a prop. "I'll say this: the stage is not in the middle of the arena, so it's not us in the round, but every seat around us, even behind us, is just as good a seat as anywhere else," Lars elaborated, as if posing the riddle of the Sphinx. "You can see the whole show from anywhere in the arena. We're selling all the way around, but we're not playing in the middle. So you figure it out."

The stage itself consisted of a diamond-shaped playing area, over which James, Jason and Kirk were free to move. The diamond cutout in the middle was the Snake Pit, where fans were sunk down below stage level, completely surrounded by the band's playing space. Arching above the Snake Pit were metal catwalks—allowing James, Jason and Kirk to play directly above the miasmic mosh-scene in the Snake Pit. On sale during the tour were T-shirts that pictured a mechanical drawing of the stage configuration.

Microphones were placed at intervals all around the stage, so James, Jason and Kirk could sing from a number of different locations. And indeed, Lars was not without mobility. With two drum kits mounted on rails, he could also move around the diamond-shaped stage. The kits rose from Snake Pit level on hydraulic lifts.

After years of touring, Lars found arenas to be "cold" places, and thought that Metallica's new configuration made the concert experience more meaningful for the fans. "As far as I know it's not written down anywhere that you have to experience a live band like that," he told *Music Express*. "We just wanted to kinda fuck with the configuration and fuck with what people are used to." Indeed, it violates a rock'n'roll fan's basic assumptions about the world to look up and see the drummer in one place—and then look up ten minutes later, to see him fifty feet away.

The diamond stage was designed to house the tour equipment during the set. Even the band's monitors were under this stage, pointed upwards so that James, Jason and Kirk could feel them booming into the soles of their feet. In addition, if Kirk, for instance, needed to get the attention of Fergie, his guitar roadie, he would have to stomp on the floor in order for the understage Fergie to get the message.

The unusually placed monitors allowed Kirk and James to get new feedback effects, and they walked around looking for "sweet spots" that created desirable feedback levels.

Aside from equipment and monitors, there is quite a bit that the audience can't see under the diamond. "I have a little table with a reading light, and those guys have made it quite cozy too," said Kirk to *Musician*. "I'm not to the point where I take newspapers down there yet, but I have seen certain band members reading scuba magazines while other guys solo." (Call it the Understage World of Lars Cousteau.)

The Snake Pit held about 120 fans or so. People would be chosen for the Snake Pit by roadies and other support personnel. Exceptionally deserving-looking or longtime fans would get passes. A vintage Misfits T-shirt might do the trick. Local radio stations would often give away the passes, which said: I WAS ON STAGE WITH METALLICA IN THE SNAKE PIT.

"It just kind of takes the normal confinements of how you're used to viewing a rock show and flushes that down the toilet," Lars told *Rip*.

What the Pitsters saw, aside from the butts of the men of Metallica, was, out of the view of the rest of the audience, a walkway that runs all around the perimeter of the Snake

Pit. On this walkway the roadies get guitars or basses ready for use—used to the curious eyes of the Snake Pit denizens.

The sound can be less than ideal for those in the Pit, and its crowded floor may have kept some from looking all the way around the stage, but it was a perspective that few Metallica fans could ever pass up. Some of the equipment storage space, and Lars's drum kit launching pads, were visible from the Snake Pit, but a thick curtain shielded most of the substage area from view.

Another ground-breaking concept that Metallica instituted during the Wherever I May Roam tour was the tapers' section. This was a designated area, usually behind the soundboard, where around a hundred selected fans could make recordings, shoot videos and snap photos to their hearts' content.

Illegally recorded concerts—bootlegs—shouldn't be confused with counterfeit copies of regularly released albums. The kind of bootlegs for which fans have spent millions of dollars for years could include unreleased studio tracks, but more often consist of amateur recordings of concerts. Many rock musicians find bootlegs to be a direct threat to their livelihood by releasing music rightfully owned by their record label. Frank Zappa chose to beat the bootleggers at their own game by taking bootleg albums, cleaning them up a tiny bit, and releasing them on his own label. With their product "stolen" by the artist, who could the bootleggers complain to? But Zappa wasn't the first musician to do this: Bob Dylan's 1975 *Basement Tapes* released a well-circulated 1967 bootleg as a two-record set.

The counterargument to the bootlegging debate says that the poor sound quality and amateurish graphics of these concert recordings don't compete with an artist's legitimate work. And the only people who'd spend their money on bootlegs, the theory goes, *already own* all the group's regularly released albums. Besides Metallica, the only other band that permits taping is the Grateful Dead. (Although musically Metallica and the Dead are more than vaguely dissimilar, they both share rabidly devoted fans.)

Aside from the aforementioned industry concerns, the band couldn't think of a good reason to forbid taping. For Lars, it was as much as issue of quality control as anything else. Allowing audience members to make their own boot-legs is an expression of sympathy for those fans who had bought poor-quality bootlegs—or even bootlegs that said "Metallica" but contained music by some other band.

"It's not really a big deal," Lars commented to *Entertainment Weekly.* "Who am I to sit on my high horse and say, 'I'm a rock star and you can't do this because it takes away from our record sales'? We don't *have* a problem with record sales."

A visit to any well-stocked collectors' record shop will certainly reveal at least twenty-five bootleg CD titles—and probably that many available on vinyl. Of cassette bootlegs there are many, many more. "I've seen lists of like 300 of our gigs that are available on tape," Lars told *Faces.* "It happens anyway, so why not put 'em in the middle, where at least it will sound better."

Lars himself had a large collection of Deep Purple and Black Sabbath bootleg videos. Lars was sometimes amazed at the amount of bootleg audio and video material hardcore Metallica fans own. As Lars concluded to *Entertainment Weekly:* "It's the ultimate souvenir to take the show home after you've lived through it.

On Wherever I May Roam, James's voice sounded stronger than it *ever* had—the result of consulting a vocal coach before the tour. This was not to try to train his voice in some

A heroic portrait of Jason at the Freddie Mercury tribute concert. *Courtesy Andrew Murray-Sipa.*

classical manner, but to try to keep from ruining it, as many other untrained singers have done.

But James just *looked* happy on that tour, offering up a savage, toothy biker-smile as he introduced "Sad but True" as "the happy song." To keep each other on their toes, James and Lars were sometimes seen spitting at each other during the set. (Heads up!)

As ever, individual solos allowed the other band members to take a quick breather. Kirk's moment in the spotlight featured a passage of electro-psycho-hillbilly riffing and a squealing metal version of Gounod's "The Funeral March of the Marionettes," better known as the theme from *Alfred Hitchcock Presents*. At the most impressive moment of his solo, Kirk kneeled at the center of the catwalk and let his ESP guitar emit a barrage of noise and pyro-delic feedback. Running down the stairs from the top of the catwalk, he dragged his instrument behind him. A roadie would then give Kirk a new, unbashed guitar for his big cadenza-ending. Banging out his last powerchord, Kirk would humbly thank the audience.

Lars's drum solo wasn't likely to make any breathtaking displays of of tub-thumping ingenuity, but rather was a sort of comic-relief break.

It was really more a drum *duet*, with James sitting down at Lars's other kit. Lars's drum also came in short bursts—with Lars feigning exhaustion after each percussive flurry. Lars had an endorsement deal with Regal Tip drumsticks, so he could feel free to toss stick after stick into the audience. Or at James. Who threw them back at Lars. Often, the two of them looked like uncoordinated jugglers tossing around very thin Indian clubs. Lars would exhort the crowd, "I guess next time I'll bring drum kits for everybody, is that a deal?" The crowd would roar in approval.

On a purely physical level, this tour affected every

band member differently. Jason claimed to sweat off three to four pounds during every show on this tour. James would be forced to use a vaporizer to keep his throat in shape if he was catching cold. And Kirk would sometimes find himself searching for a pickle first thing in the morning—for use as a hangover cure.

Because of James's occasional skateboarding accidents, rumors were afloat that this most recent Metallica tour contract included a "no skateboarding" clause. It didn't. However, the band was doing its best to survive its sometimes dangerous hobbies. Kirk had been spending more time mountain-biking than skateboarding, and told *Thrasher,* "The good thing about mountain bikes is they have brakes."

The $15 *Wherever I May Roam* glossy-stock tour book is pitch black, with the coiled "Don't Tread on Me" snake in raised graphics. Filled with color and black-and-white photographs of the band, the book also includes bits of album reviews, letters about Metallica to metal magazines and comments from fellow musicians. They are all uniformly negative, accusing the band of selling out, of being pro-war, of being bad musicians and a host of other professional and personal transgressions. It was a decidedly self-deprecating—and highly self-confident—move on the band's part.

Instead of an opening band, the tour featured a movie to warm up the crowd. According to Lars, the idea for a short movie as an introduction was taken from the 1990 Paul McCartney tour that opened with a Richard Lester–directed film.

"The movie gets everybody pumped up," Lars told *Faces.* "There's some pretty cool, as well as weird, stuff on there about what we've been up to for the last ten years."

The thirty-minute movie that preceded the shows includes just-shot video footage of the town the band was playing in, as well as scenes of kids entering the arena that same evening. (Whenever this just-shot video of that evening's fans were shown on the big screen, pockets of recognition were marked by screams all over the arena.) Live feeds from the dressing room show the band members getting ready for the concert with words of encouragement for their ecstatic fans. Such electronic props don't come cheap, though. Anyone who thinks that Metallica saved money by not having an opening band, James was quick to point out, doesn't realize just how much a video crew costs the tour.

Sometimes backed by baroque music, the Metallica movie also features footage of the WEA pressing plant turning out Metallica discs, slow-motion footage of the band in concert, and an interview with Lars about the old days and Cliff Burton, followed by a sort of mini-Cliff tribute.

Excerpts of MTV interviews with Metallica fans are also included. When asked by MTV why he likes Metallica, one fan replies elegantly, "Because they're better."

Images of past tours fly by, with pictures of Doris the Justice goddess disassembled for transit and falling apart in concert. Bits of previous videos are also compiled in the film, including snippets from the studio-shot *Metallica Sessions 1990–1991*. It even includes further footage of Kip Winger's dart attacks in the One on One studio.

But when the screen goes to Clint Eastwood in *The Good, the Bad, and the Ugly*, the fans' hysteria surges. They know that Metallica is about to take the stage. With Ennio Morricone's "Ecstasy of Gold" rising ecclesiastically above the crowd, enough lighters are lit to turn the arena into a crowded galaxy of flickering yellow stars.

Sets during the Wherever I May Roam tour began with

flash pots marking the beginning of "Enter Sandman." James's rendition of "Sad but True" was filled with exhortations to sing along. Beginning with its taped sitar intro, "Wherever I May Roam" was the song on the tour most often dropped when time restrictions made the band shave their set a bit.

For "The Unforgiven," James's Gibson Chet Atkins acoustic/electric guitar hung from the mike stand. Throughout the song, James switched back and forth between that guitar and his regular, custom-made ESP.

To prove that the *Justice* songs aren't universally rejected, the Wherever tour features a version of "Harvester of Sorrow" that includes such a pregnant pause that most listeners think that the song is over. Sometimes called "riff-arama," a medley of *Justice* songs "Blackened" and ". . . And Justice for All" would last just over seven minutes—not long enough for anyone in the audience to get that droopy, long-song face. Lars thought that the overlong *Justice* material sounded better in medley form, but joked that Metallica must be getting old, now that they've started putting together medleys.

Older tunes represented on the tour included "Whiplash," "For Whom the Bell Tolls," "Welcome Home (Sanitarium)," "Orion," and "Creeping Death," the latter with its infectious fist-pumping sing-along chant of "DIE!" When the beat would kick in on "Fade to Black," flashpots would explode with the white-hot intensity of magnesium flares.

(Not all oldies work out so well. At one Albany, New York, show, the band played a couple of minutes of "Fight Fire with Fire," but soon fell apart. That was all they could remember of that one, they offered in their defense.)

The band's encore setlist included "Master of Puppets" and "Damage, Inc.," along with an extended version of "Seek and Destroy" that allowed James to wade out into the audience, getting people to sing along with the song's three-word chorus. As ever, knowing all the words was a Metallica fan's first duty. "Check and see if your buddy don't know it," James would scream to the crowd.

"One" began with flashpots replicating World War I battlefield noises. First scattered, then more rapid-fire, ultimately flash pots would be exploding all over the stage. And out of the drifting smoke would walk James, Kirk, Jason—with Lars rising up on his levitating drumset.

Mostly saved for encores, Metallica cover tunes included "Am I Evil?," "Stone Cold Crazy" and "The Last Caress." For an instant, they would play a famous melody from Grieg's "Hall of the Mountain King," or maybe an old Deep Purple riff. On rare occasions, the band would cover Aerosmith's "Walk This Way" and ZZ Top's "La Grange." They weren't skillfully played, but none of these oddball covers ever ran any more than a couple of verses. But when they played Black Sabbath's "Iron Man" with Lars singing and James on drums, they somehow managed to get through most of the song.

Following Metallica's first mainstream hit album, the Wherever I May Roam tour brought in a lot of first-time (and often very young) fans. For the parents accompanying their kids to the show, the Capital Centre in Washington, D.C., provided a "quiet room" where they could wait out the show far away from those nasty headbangers in relative peace and quiet. In the San Jose Mercury News, Kirk had a message for parents: "Tell them they will be perfectly safe at the show. Metallica is a great baby-sitter. Just remember to bring the ear plugs. Even we wear them."

To James, the new crowds lacked the cultish intensity of the old days. "A lot of the audience is no doubt watered-down," he told Melody Maker. "There's a lot of people there just because, 'Oooo, play "Enter Sandman." ' So we play it first to get the fucking thing out of the way. So they have to sit through the rest of the shit! They gotta hear the old shit. You gotta use it against them, y'know? But we're teachin' 'em!"

Nothing annoys the Metallicans more than the suggestion that wider popularity means they've sold out. "The only thing we're selling out is arenas," Lars snapped at *The New York Times*. "I know that's the stupid answer but I'm defensive. I've heard that kind of stuff since we put a ballad on *Ride the Lightning* in 1984."

Just as the stylistic departures of *Ride the Lightning* alienated some, the big-beat, groove-oriented *Metallica* was also bound to raise the hackles of self-described "purists." When a supposedly underground genre such as thrash finds a popular audience, the obscurists seem let down. Perhaps all it means, as Lars remarked to the *Atlanta Journal-Constitution*, was that "We seem to be the accepted of the unacceptable."

23

> Tonight Metallica
> rules the rock and
> roll universe.
> Metallica Alcohollica.
> One Nation Under
> Alloy. Nicky sings the
> lyrics to "Disposable
> Heroes"—"*I was
> born for dying*" —a
> grunt's antiwar song.
> Nicky and Mingo
> joke around. "This
> music kills kids!
> Listen to the lyrics!"
> Then they confess
> they'd die without it.
>
> —Donna Gaines,
> *Teenage Wasteland*

Proud to be rockers, the men of Metallica are reluctant to be artists. But just like great artists, Metallica takes our world from us and hands it back in a new shape. Metallica sings words that have never been sung before, plays riffs that have never been played before, and raises questions that would never have been raised had a teenaged Lars Ulrich not gotten this urge to start a band.

"A lot of times I get uncomfortable in interviews if I'm asked to over-analyze the whole thing, because I'm not sure the whole thing's supposed to be analyzed," Lars commented to Harold DeMuir. "We just do it, and I'm not really sure if it's right to sit and analyze what the whole thing is about. I'm not sure if it's really *worth* analyzing that much. Maybe it is, but maybe it isn't."

If Metallica really were artists, it wouldn't turn them into clownish bohemians or bitchy fops—after all, they've always been part-band, part-*béorscipe*. And yet, to *Metal*

Kirk at Wembley. *Courtesy Andrew Murray-Sipa.*

Forces, Lars puzzled over the fact that mainstream press outlets such as *Rolling Stone* and *Time* magazines thought of Metallica as the "Thinking Man's Heavy Metal band. We are seen by them as a serious band, and all they want to talk about are the profound implications of our lyrics! Personally, I think it is too one-sided. I wish they would lighten up on us a little and talk about the other sides to the band. We are still doing our debauchery, getting drunk and waking up with the same hangovers as we've always had. I wish the media would put over that side of our personalities as well."

While recording *Metallica,* the marriages of Lars, Jason and Kirk all ended in divorce. Kirk remembered the three band members hanging around during rehearsal, sighing woefully over their private lives. They then realized that they were all going through the same thing. That they all had problems simultaneously was coincidental, but their personal crises made them aware of one thing: the stabilizing factor that Metallica had become for their lives.

In some respects, Metallica never stops being Metallica—they won't turn it off, because there's no reason to. "We're not exactly the type of band who come off tour and hide away in Scotland for ages," Lars told *Metallix*. "People can always find us, they'll always know where we are and what we're doing, because we're still the same drunken idiots we always were."

Drunken idiots who've spoken their minds in hundreds of interviews, sometimes about *real* subjects, too. Kirk Hammett is a fervent believer in women's reproductive rights. "A woman should be able to make her own decisions whether or not she should have a baby," he told *Metallix*. "She should have control over her body, not the fucking government, congressmen or whatever."

And as the risk of AIDS lurked in the hotel rooms of touring rock bands—especially with the still-active groupie-based backstage sexual barter system—James Hetfield commented to *Creem Metal*: "This shit scares me. You know, one time and you're dead!! Touring is the dangerous part. A lot of bands are going to be in trouble the way they carry on. I mean, we've been pretty bad, but on the last tour, no way! It was kinda like, 'Screw that!' " Despite the self-contradictory nature of James's final remark, millions of metalheads hope he and Metallica follow his advice.

The footprint of Metallica was so broad against the back of heavy metal, it's hard to assess their contributions. "It's just mind-boggling, really," recalls their old friend Brian Slagel. "When you think about where it began, none of us at the time ever thought any of this was gonna get as big as it has.

It's just amazing. Metallica is one of the two biggest bands in the world right now. And they've had an effect, not just on the metal scene, but on the music scene in general. They've kept the fire burning and made it burn brighter."

Naturally, Lars takes the reductive approach, by starting with what he *doesn't* like. "To me, the most boring thing in the world is safe, mainstream heavy metal. . . . I'd rather listen to Madonna," he told Harold DeMuir. "I think we're different. We've taken what we started and opened it up, without losing the basis of what we were doing originally, adding new influences and finding new things to write about. We keep getting more experience as musicians, and our music keeps expanding. It's a challenge to make some of this shit interesting, instead of always taking the easy way out. It's so easy to do verse/chorus/verse/chorus/fade-three-times-on-the-third-chorus/see ya. Easy, but fuckin' *boring,* you know?"

Heavy metal preconceptions die hard, despite Metallica's best efforts. While doing a photo shoot for the British rock weekly *Melody Maker,* the photographer had the idea to pose the band in "tough" metal poses, such as in heroic formation, or behind metal bars. Lars informed him that Metallica wouldn't.

Lars made his feeling known about preconceived genres to *Melody Maker*: "When people ask me, 'What's the most suitable tag for your music?' I tell them we got a band name. That's so people can recognize us as different from any other band. We're Metallica."

Somehow unwilling to acknowledge Metallica's primacy in the new metal of the eighties, Lars believed the only *real* revolution in metal was the NWOBHM.

In fulfillment of what must have been a decade-long dream, Lars Ulrich compiled an album of his favorite NWOBHM songs for release by PolyGram in the United

Kingdom and Metal Blade in the United States. The hitch: Lars would have to track down all these bands himself. "I would hear the stories from Lars—it was very difficult," Brian remembers. "I think he went into it thinking, 'I'll get a list of songs together, I'll give it to the PolyGram legal people in London and they'll contact the people and get the songs and it'll be really simple.' But as it turned out, number one, finding some of these people was a nightmare because most of these bands had just disintegrated and the guys were working regular day-jobs and had just vanished from London."

Some NWOBHM artists, no matter how many years they'd spent in obscurity, would still manage to give Lars a hard time as he tried to repopularize their music. As Brian Slagel remembers, "Every few months, we would talk and the subject would come up and he'd go, 'Oh, God, here's the story about this one.' And I'd say 'Man, you're in Hell!' What was supposed to be this nice little fun project turned out to be kind of hellish. But in the end I think it came out really good and I'm really happy he did it."

The title NWOBHM New Wave of British Heavy Metal '79 Revisited has a rather Metallic ring, and a quick perusal reveals the original versions of famed covers "Helpless" and "Blitzkrieg." The retrospective, comprising twenty-four tracks, included early songs from such well-known metal bands as Def Leppard and Iron Maiden, as well as seldom-heard legends like Trespass, Angel Witch, Tygers of Pang Tang and Witchfynde. Geoff Barton, coiner of the term NWOBHM and editor of Kerrang!, also contributed to the liner notes.

NWOBMH is overrun with supreme riffsmanship, especially from Diamond Head, Sweet Savage, Blitzkrieg, Holocaust, Weapon, Paradox, Jaguar, Tygers of Pang Tang, Gaskin, Angel Witch and Vardis. Influences on Metallica are easy to hear, from the different sections and rhythm changes of Samson's "Vice Versa" to Trespass's "One of These Days," with its hooky instrumental rhapsodies.

During the summer of 1991, as Metallica was still finishing *Metallica,* the *other* children of the NWOBHM were getting together for one massive tour. Cooked up by Jon Zazula of Megaforce, Megadeth manager Ron Laffitte and Slayer honcho Rick Sales, the highly successful Clash of the Titans tour would bring together the greats of the genre that dares not call itself "thrash": Anthrax, Megadeth, Slayer and slowcore opener Alice in Chains (for kids with little or no high-speed moshing experience).

Metal styles have always ebbed and flowed, changing to suit the times. "Five years ago, Journey was metal," James once remarked to *Guitar Player.* "Now, there are all sorts of stereotypes: speedcore, thrash, or fuckin' death-super-Satan metal. It's really ridiculous." (During a 1986 interview with *Sounds,* James interjected, "Tell 'em we're jazz-metal." To which Cliff Burton added, "Yeah, we're thrash-jazz.")

New genres are being mated, combined and recombined every day. Heavy metal had become some sort of long-haired biotech lab. The metal world, ripped open by the mold-smashing metal of Metallica, is now swamped with a host of crossbreeds: Primus, Faith No More, Soundgarten, Nirvana, Ministry, Alice in Chains, whatever . . .

Black music would also feel the gravitational pull of the new metal. Rapper and professed Metallica fan Ice-T knocked together gangsta rap and thrash-metal for his controversial band Body Count.

Regardless of how they felt about each other, metal and rap knew they were equal in society's disapproval of them. At Def Jam Records, Rick Rubin featured a Slayer sample in a Public Enemy song. Rick Rubin was also involved with the historic rap/rock teaming of Run-DMC and Aerosmith for "Walk This Way." Suburban kids Run-DMC created the first rap-metal crossover when wailing guitars met syncopated rhymes on their 1984 single "Rock Box."

Ultimately, agit-prop rappers Public Enemy burst onto the thrash world with their Anthrax duet "Bring the Noise." Realizing they shared a common philosophical base, the two (seeming) polar opposites went out on the road with Primus and Young Black Teenagers.

Metal continues to stratify itself into increasingly "underground" genres. The late eighties saw a blossoming of the new extreme form of metal, grindcore. Based predominantly in England, grindcore takes the horror-movie predilictions of the Mifsits or W.A.S.P. and focuses almost exclusively on their grossest aspects. The riffing is fast and tangled—the vocals little more than rasping drones. Sometimes called "medi-core" for their graphic depictions of blood and guts, these bands include Napalm Death, Carcass, Entombed, Confessor and others, the majority of which are signed to the British Earache label.

On April 20, 1992, Metallica took part in a rock concert whose audience was global—the AIDS-awareness tribute to Freddie Mercury, the Queen lead vocalist who had succumbed to the virus the year before. Held at London's Wembley Stadium, the concert featured the diverse talents of Guns n' Roses, Def Leppard, Robert Plant, Roger Daltrey, David Bowie, Seal, Elton John, Annie Lennox, Lisa Stansfield, George Michael and, incredibly, Liza Minnelli. Remaining Queen members Brian May, John Deacon and Roger Taylor said that the purpose of the concert was to give Freddie Mercury "the biggest send-off in history."

And the first band up for the biggest send-off in history? Metallica. With a crowd of 72,000, the immense Wembley Stadium was filled to overflowing, an image reminiscent of an old Warner Bros. cartoon scene. The Metallicans launched into "Enter Sandman" and the cartoon crowd turned into a sea of rocking fists.

Their second song was "Sad but True," allowing Jason to demonstrate to this all-ages audience what real headbanging was all about. On the tune, Kirk mangled his guitar against a wall of Marshalls, throwing himself into the song's ritualistic frenzy.

The band's third and final song was the crowd-pleasing slow-dance number "Nothing Else Matters." James briefly thanked Queen, and Metallica disappeared hastily, not wanting to screw up the scheduling for the rest of the concert.

Later on in the tribute, James joined the three last Queen members onstage for a version of "Stone Cold Crazy." Noticeably thrilled to be onstage with his old heroes, James stalked about grinning and grimacing.

With nary a minute to take their snapshots to the drugstore from the Wherever I May Roam tour, Metallica picked up and hit the road during the summer of '92 with hard-rock heavyweights Guns n' Roses and openers Faith No More. The tour was announced at a Los Angeles press conference presided over by Lars and Slash.

A scenic trek across America's loveliest fifty-thousand-person-capacity stadiums, the Metallica/GNR road show played over twenty dates, starting July 17 in RFK Stadium, Washington, D.C. It snaked its way to such venerable venues as Giants Stadium in New Jersey, the Silverdome in Detroit, the Hoosier Dome in Indianapolis and the 100,000-seat Rose Bowl. Each band played sets of over two hours each—which afforded Metallica enough breathing space to expand on their Golden Hits festival formula.

The two bands had always been good friends, and

had long discussed a joint tour. Lars always thought it was a good idea: Metallica likes to go on early and GNR likes to go on late. James for one assumed that Metallica would already be passed out cold by the time the Guns n' Roses set began.

For Metallica's portion of the show, the small photographers' pit in front of the stage was put to use as a kind of improvised snake pit. Banners flanked the stage, each bearing a recognizably Pusheadian weather-beaten skull.

Metallica's set had changed a bit from the Wherever I May Roam tour that preceded it. Their new version of "Master of Puppets" was shortened, stripped of its pretty guitar-harmony middle-section. "Am I Evil?" was even more drastically shortened. *Justice* nugget "The Shortest Straw" was dusted off, although James usually offered his own caveats before the band tackled its vexing changes. They performed most of *Metallica*, as well as favorites "Fade to Black," "Seek and Destroy," "Whiplash" and set-closer "One," accompanied by enough flash pots to bring back 1918 all over again.

Jason's bass solos would throw in bits of "The Star-Spangled Banner" and Led Zeppelin's "Dazed and Confused." Kirk would later join Jason for viciously rocking, acidic duets.

Fans and reviewers alike were impressed by Metallica's frenzy-building energy and rock'n'roll professionalism, while GN'R's Axl Rose tended to make news for his late appearances and even later-running sets. Rose also faced recurring throat problems that forced the postponement of dates in Toronto, Denver, San Diego, Minneapolis, Columbia, South Carolina and Foxboro, Massachusetts. But before long, the Metallicans found themselves sidelined as well.

During Metallica's August 8 appearance at Montreal's Olympic Stadium, James got too close to an exploding flash pot and suffered first- and second-degree burns on his face, arms and hands. The back of his left hand even showed the charred signs of the third-degree burn. He was immediately rushed to a local hospital. (Later, Lars told MTV News that James had been "engulfed in flames for about a full second" and that it had been "a miracle" that his injuries weren't more serious.)

Things only went downhill from there at Olympic Stadium. Shocked by James's accident and upset that Metallica's set was cut short, the Montreal crowd was hoping that a rousing G'NR ruckus would pick their spirits back up. Unfortunately, Axl Rose's trouble-prone throat was once again below form, and he cut the concert short.

Though bitterly disappointed, most of the stadium's fifty-three thousand fans filed out peacefully. But a crowd of two thousand were not the least bit peaceful. They reportedly set small fires, broke seats and windows, overturned cars and even clashed violently with police. The police, around two hundred in number, chased down fans with billy clubs and even lobbed tear gas into Olympic Stadium itself.

When the fracas was over, three police officers and ten fans had received minor injuries and there were twelve arrests. The damage to the facility was reported to have cost an estimated $300,000 to $400,000.

After James's accident and the melee in Montreal, more tour dates had to be pushed back. Venues in Seattle, Oakland, and Pasadena, California, were rescheduled without much problem. (Only the B.C. Place stadium in Vancouver proved an exception. As autumn approached, it's field was monopolized by football games.) Rescheduling ran the tour well into September, which conflicted with Faith No More, whose own headlining tour began on the fifteenth of that month.

With James recovering from his burns, new guitarists

were auditioned for his parts. Ultimately, their choice for substitute rhythm guitarist was their old friend Jim Marshall from Metal Church.

Metallica returned to the tour during the last week of August 1992 at the International Speedway in Jason's hometown of Phoenix, Arizona. James's doctors weren't ready to let James pick up a guitar again, so he sang to Jim Marshall's accompaniment. At least the Metallica/Guns n' Roses/Faith No More road show was rolling again.

How can one measure Metallica's fame? What can mean more than Grammy awards, platinum albums or arena attendance records? Only one thing: being made into a comic book.

Revolutionary Comics of San Diego published two comic books about—and starring—Metallica. The comic was utterly unauthorized by the band, for all of Revolutionary Comics' rock-band stories are unauthorized. (But comic aficionado Kirk must certainly have gotten some small thrill from collecting his own comic.)

The story line of the *Metallica II* comic charted the band's career from the release of ... *And Justice for All* through the Long Beach fracas up to the release of *Metallica*. Supposed issues between band members are dramatized in moderately good comic-book art. (In a few frames, Jason bore a bit too close a resemblance to Zippy the Pinhead for him to feel particularly flattered.) The band's dialogue is often taken from press interviews, and a lot of care was taken to give these comics the ring of authenticity. Still, one can't help but feel disappointed that these comics don't have Metallica battling supernatural, essence-draining, winged, fire-pit wraiths. (Now *that* one Kirk would've collected *and read*.)

Fame, as Metallica often discovered, is goofy. While

on an MTV call-in show with icon-of-eighties-blandness Martha Quinn, Lars and Kirk gave in to the inherent humor of the situation. In fact, their sense of absurdity was welling up in them like a violent sneeze—the kind of feeling that led Cliff Burton to crack up at an interviewer's feeble question all those years before.

"People say, 'Do you realize how successful you are and how much impact you have?' I say, 'See ya!' "
—Lars Ulrich (*Circus*)

"Some guy was bowing to me at the Marquee the other night, seriously! And I was shouting at him, 'Stop it—let me buy you a beer.' "
—James Hetfield (*Faces Rocks*)

Metallica has indeed become the most important metal band around. With their mugs plastered all over the world, the Metallicans still enjoy going into public places. This usually amounts to a full load of autograph duty, but they aren't about to complain. You could hear them saying, *"Yeah, sure I'll sign it—too bad you don't have a camera . . ."*

James occasionally seeks refuge in country-oriented bars, where his anonmymity can be reasonably assured. Strip clubs continue to count as favorite hangouts for reasons of privacy and other, slightly more libidinous, impulses. But isn't Metallica always to be found on the frayed ends of society?

"The only thing that I worry about is that, when you travel from luxury hotel to luxury hotel, and your tour manager pays all your bills, it can get very comfortable and you can lose some of your hunger," Lars told Harold DeMuir. "If we lose that hunger and that eagerness, then we could be in serious trouble. Obviously we're comfortable, and I'm not gonna sit here and say that we don't enjoy having money, but we have to seriously watch out that we don't get *too* comfortable, because I have a feeling that that could fuck us up."

"*Metallica is going to be one of the bands you look back on in the year 2008, that people will still listen to the way I still listen to Zeppelin and Sabbath albums.*"

—Jason Newsted (*Rolling Stone*)

"*Metallica's the only band I've ever been in. I'm not sure that when it ends in five, ten years, I'm going to put an ad in the paper saying, 'Stupid drummer looking for stupid people to play music with.' Metallica is it and I think when that ceases, that's it.*"

—Lars Ulrich (*Melody Maker*)

Lars rocks Wembley: "Metallica is *it*. When that ceases, that's it." *Courtesy Andrew Murray-Sipa.*

D I S C O G R A P H Y*

ALBUMS

Kill 'Em All (Megaforce), 1983

Ride the Lightning (Megaforce), 1984

Ride the Lightning (Elektra), 1984

Master of Puppets (Elektra), 1986

Kill 'Em All (Elektra), 1986 (includes "Am I Evil?" and "Blitzkrieg")

. . . And Justice for All (Elektra), 1988

Metallica (Elektra), 1991

Metallica (CBS/Sony), 1991 (includes "So What?")

EPs

Jump in the Fire (Vertigo), 1983 (includes live versions of "Seek and Destroy" and "Phantom Lord")

---

*For reasons of preserving author sanity, this discography includes only regularly released Metallica records from the U.S., England or Japan. Whether these releases appear on CD, CD3, cassette or vinyl has not been noted. No promotional-only releases are included, nor are picture discs, interview discs, gold anniversary twelve-inch discs, limited-edition boxed sets or any collector's package that includes T-shirts, badges, patches, bandannas, storage units, bumper stickers, prints, chains, Doris figurines, snake figurines or anything else the hardcore Metallica fan could desire.

Creeping Death (Vertigo), 1984 (includes "Am I Evil?" and "Blitzkrieg")

Creeping Death/Jump in the Fire (Vertigo), 1984 (both preceding EPs together)

Whiplash (Megaforce), 1985 (includes live versions of "Seek and Destroy" and "Phantom Lord")

Harvester of Sorrow (Vertigo), 1988 (includes non-album tracks)

The $5.98 EP: Garage Days Rerevisited (Elektra), 1987 (CD version titled *The $9.98 CD: Garage Days Rerevisited*)

One (Vertigo), 1989 (includes live version of "For Whom the Bell Tolls" and "Welcome Home [Sanitarium]")

One (CBS/Sony), 1989 (includes "Breadfan," the "One" demo, and live versions of "Welcome Home [Sanitarium]" and "For Whom the Bell Tolls")

Enter Sandman (Vertigo), 1991 (includes "Stone Cold Crazy" and the "Enter Sandman" demo)

The Unforgiven (Vertigo), 1991 (includes "Killing Time" and demo of "The Unforgiven")

Nothing Else Matters (Vertigo), 1992 (includes the "Nothing Else Matters" demo and live versions of "Enter Sandman" and "Harvester of Sorrow")

Nothing Else Matters (Vertigo), 1992 (includes "Enter Sandman," "Sad but True" and "Nothing Else Matters" from the Wembley Stadium Freddie Mercury concert)

SINGLES

"One" b/w "The Prince," 1988

"Eye of the Beholder" b/w "Breadfan," 1988

"Enter Sandman" b/w "Stone Cold Crazy," 1991

"The Unforgiven" b/w "Killing Time," 1991

"Nothing Else Matters" b/w "Enter Sandman" (live), 1992

"Sad but True" b/w "So What?", 1992

COMPILATION CUTS

"Hit the Lights," from *Metal Massacre* (Metal Blade), 1981

"Stone Cold Crazy," from *Rubaiyat* (Elektra), 1990

V I D E O G R A P H Y

$19.98 Home Vid Cliff 'Em All! (Elektra Entertainment), 1987

2 of One (Elektra Entertainment), 1989

For Those About to Rock (Warner Home Video), 1992 (with AC/DC, the Black Crowes and Pantera)

A Year and a Half in the Life of Metallica Part 1 (Elektra Entertainment), 1992

A Year and a Half in the Life of Metallica. . . Continued Part 2 (Elektra Entertainment), 1992